CAPE FEAR TECHNICAL INSTITUTE
Property of Library
Cape Fear Technical Institute
Wilmington, N. C.

NORTH CAROLINA
STATE BOARD
DEPT. OF COMMERCE
LIBRARIES

P9-DNS-151

Home Gardener's Cookbook

DISCARD

DISCARD

DISCARD

DISCA

Home Gardener's Cookbook

Marjorie Page Blanchard

ILLUSTRATED BY

Carole Cole Goldsborough

GARDEN WAY PUBLISHING COMPANY
Charlotte, Vermont 05455

DISCARD

DISCARD

All rights reserved—no part of this book may be reproduced in any form without permission in writing from the publisher, except by reviewer who wishes to quote brief passages in connection with a review written for inclusion in magazine or newspaper.

Library of Congress Catalog Card Number: 73-89129
ISBN 0-88266-013-6 paperback
ISBN 0-88266-014-4 casebound

COPYRIGHT 1974 BY GARDEN WAY PUBLISHING CO.
CHARLOTTE, VERMONT 05445

Printed in the United States

Contents

INTRODUCTION, 7

A book for the gardener and the cook, who are not necessarily one and the same person.

JANUARY, 9

Fireside planning of the garden while the seed catalogs begin to arrive. Choosing the best varieties to order. Winter recipes from last year's garden.

FEBRUARY, 27

Plans for the garden and perhaps a small orchard and fruit garden. Planning the soil's preparation. Recipes for wintered-over stores, like carrots, kale and leeks.

MARCH, 39

The seed packets arrive and, if the sun smiles, early peas may be sown. Make plans for the herb garden. Try some special maple recipes.

APRIL, 45

The time—and the ways—for planting peas and onions, first crops of lettuces and the root vegetables, parsley and cress. Recipes for fresh dandelion greens, for watercress.

MAY, 51

Now make short plantings of chard and lettuce, radishes and carrots. The pea fence goes up, and in go broccoli, cabbage and pepper plants. Feast on new asparagus and on rhubarb, too.

JUNE, 65

Small radishes, lettuces, carrots and beans are ready. Re-plant them as you pick. Gorge on the fresh peas and the new strawberries. It's time, too, for salads, young beets with their greens, fresh herbs with meats and in jellies.

JULY, 91

Plant more succession crops while you cope with the pests. For rewards here are the new blueberries, cherries, currants and raspberries, fresh from the garden and in pies, cakes and cordials.

AUGUST, 129

The garden, now on its own, yields its greatest gifts for celery Amandine, cauliflower Polonaise, stuffed cabbage, chilled cucumber soup, eggplant Parmesan, baked onions, new potatoes Savoyarde, maple limas, corn timbales, or perhaps a colache of zucchinis, onion, corn, peppers and red tomatoes.

SEPTEMBER, 159

As the bounty wanes it's time for a garden clean-up and to plant a few late crops. Here's the season of the wine-baked peaches, plum trifles, curried melon, apple turnovers, fruit-filled pears and Concord grape pie. Or try a new recipe for red cabbage or braised turnips.

OCTOBER, 181

The first frost blackens vines, the signal for putting the garden to bed, for setting tools away—and for the final fall harvest of nutty winter squashes, pumpkins for Hallowe'en and to go into breads and custards, for late chard dishes and popcorn balls. Now the garden rests. The gardener too, while dreaming of next year.

INDEX, 191

Introduction

THIS IS a book for the vegetable gardener and the cook—who are not necessarily one and the same person. It is a putting down on paper of the logical sequence of events in a gardener's year, from the time the seed catalogs arrive until the last vegetables are harvested. It tells you how much to order, how many rows to plant, when to plant and when to pick. The amounts are based on the needs of the average family of four, give or take the personal likes and dislikes that we all encounter. Planting dates are from the author's experiences in southern Connecticut, so time must be shortened or lengthened according to other geographical locations.

For the cook, I have tried to provide inspiration for the preparation of all of your garden produce recommended here, with new ideas and pleasant reminders of old ones.

Most important to both cook and gardener is the pleasure and enjoyment that should be part of having a vegetable garden; the creativity involved in planning and planting, picking and preparing the bountiful harvest that begins in the bleakness of winter, comes to fruition in the heat of summer, and ends as the trees shed their leaves once again.

January

UNDER A notation entitled "strawberries in the snow," my garden diary reminds me that the first catalog arrived January fifth.

What a welcome sight it is, and even the mailman is cheered. By this time we gardeners have long since recovered from the finality and relief of putting the garden to bed. We have, like everyone else, celebrated a long holiday season highlighted by gifts from our pantry shelves. We are, to be honest, experiencing a certain restlessness. No long winter's nap for us. And the imaginative men who put together picture-book seed catalogs know their gardening customers well. We may not order until February, but we want our literature now.

We want to dream of "greener pastures" with every vegetable looking like its catalog picture. We want to plan, whether it be our first garden or our twenty-first. And that is what this book is all about: the planning of your planting, your picking, and your preparation of the fruits and vegetables from your own garden and orchard. It is an in-season book designed to see you through the garden year, with emphasis on planning ahead so that your crops and your appetite for them are synchronized—with allowances for the frailties of Nature and of ourselves.

A vegetable garden is never completed; it is constantly changing with the discovery of new types of produce or new methods of planting. And a vegetable gardener is never content with the status quo. Even in the midst of the growing season I often catch myself saying, "Now, next year . . ." That is part of the reason for being a gardener. It challenges creativity and keeps us alert mentally and physically. There is a never-ending cycle to growing, and we learn to harmonize with Nature's moods and profit from our own errors.

If you are reading this book, you must be interested in the garden and what it produces. I don't have to sell you on the advantages of having the freshest flavors, the tiniest beans, the sweetest corn, marble-sized beets and potatoes, individual eggplants. You know the joys of growing and the therapy for tired spirits of digging in the dirt until you feel renewed and refreshed. You know the fun of going out into the raspberry patch at sunrise and picking berries still sparkling with dew for the breakfast table; the excitement on the day that the pea pods are full enough to eat; the sweet buttery flavor of raw zucchini picked three inches long with the blossom still on it. These are some of the answers to "Why have a vegetable garden?" What and when and how takes a bit longer, and we'll take each step as it comes.

I would like to stroll through a vegetable garden in the order of planting, with suggestions as to the amounts and varieties needed to have a healthy and hearty source of nutritional pleasure throughout the season. Remember, this is based on the likes, dislikes, and appetites of a family of four.

PEAS are the first crop to be planted. You'll do it in March if you can; otherwise put them in as soon as you can turn over the ground. We like *Lincoln* because in our area of southeastern Connecticut they have never failed us. *Little Marvel* and *Sparkle* also are good producers. Generally, peas do not like

hot weather, so one early planting that will mature in about seventy days will have to do. There is one type that is reputed to stand heat—*Wando*—which can be planted as late as July first and will produce about the middle of September. But because we like the space for something else as soon as the early peas are through, we put in a two-row planting as early as practical. We buy a pound of peas and plant two 32-foot rows, one row

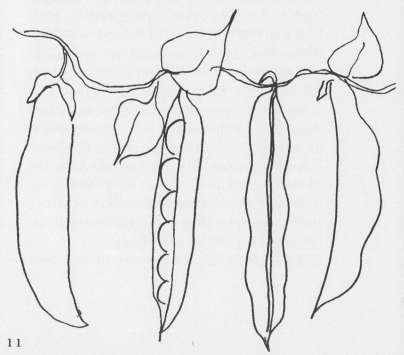

as early as possible, one later in April. We finish off the packets by planting the rest around the edge of the garden so they can climb the fence. Presuming that they all germinate—and they usually do—we can eat our fill for a couple of weeks in every form— hot, cold, creamed, in soup, in salad—and still freeze enough to carry us through March. I'll have to admit that I don't waste our good garden peas on all of the visiting children who prefer Birdseye anyhow. I'll leave that part of their education to their own mothers.

RADISHES come in many varieties. *Champion* and *Cherry Belle* are two of the common ones. You could try the *Icicle* which has a milder flavor and is the earliest long white radish. For winter use there is a *Black Spanish* to plant in July and August, but it lacks the "bite" of the summer radish. And what is a radish without its bite? Radishes mature quickly—in about four weeks—so you can sow them every two weeks except in midsummer, for they do not like hot weather. Two packets will see you through.

CARROTS are surely one of the most popular garden vegetables for growing, though eating may be another matter. Try various types: *Nantes, Chantenay, Pioneer* or a short and sweet variety called *Oxheart* which is recommended for heavy soil because it is broad and only 4½ inches long. One ounce of seed is more than enough, but there will be some waste in planting, as carrot seeds are so tiny. You will want to plant every three weeks throughout the summer and as late as the end of August to keep a steady supply coming in and to insure having them small in size.

BEETS are delicious when small but tend to become woody if they are let go. You can have a pretty platter of young carrots and golf ball-sized beets, as they both come in at about the same time. Sow beets thinly and transplant your thinnings. Plant for the first time in April; plant again in June and again in August, or up to within six weeks of the first killing frost in your area. Beets are easy to grow and don't attract insects or disease. If you don't like them, my advice is: learn to. *Crosby, Detroit Dark Red* and *Ruby Queen* are all good. There is a new golden beet that is delicious and unusual and does not bleed like the red. Try a few just for fun.

PARSNIPS are old-fashioned, humble, and beloved by those who know them well. They evoke memories of family dinners long past, although the present generation may not have any such memories because the parsnips gets short shrift these days. They do take a long time to grow—about four months—but that is why they're an excellent late fall and winter crop. Plant them in late spring if you have cold winters, in early fall if you have mild winters. *Harris Model, All American* and *Hollow Crown* are all good, and one packet is enough for a fifteen-foot row.

The LETTUCES in any catalog are mesmerizing! How to choose? Shall it be *Buttercrunch, Cos, Black Seeded Simpson, Ruby, Salad Bowl, Oakleaf* or *Boston?* Actually we often plant all of these varieties because that is one reason for growing our own. The *Cos* (or *Romaine*) will do well all summer and on into fall. The leaf lettuces *(Buttercrunch,*

Simpson, Boston) should be pulled as soon as they reach maturity or become large full heads, because they will develop a bitter flavor if left in the ground. Successive sowings are very important with lettuce, and you should start out with small amounts. We just divide two 32-foot rows into equal parts for our first planting and put in approximately ten feet of each type. Plant every three weeks and finish off the summer with a planting of *Romaine* about the third week in August.

Do plan to plant SPINACH. It is really the most maligned vegetable in the whole garden catalog, and for generations no one has cooked it properly. Even Popeye didn't help its popularity. Plant it because, if for no other reason, it is the first thing to come up in the spring and a few green spinach leaves in a salad or an omelet are a tonic in themselves. Spinach is fast-growing and demands cool weather. It should be planted in early spring and then again in late summer. I like to plant quite a bit—a 28-foot row—and harvest it all at once. Then forget spinach and use chard throughout the summer and go back to spinach in the fall. *Blooms-dale Long-Standing* is an old favorite. *New Zealand* is not a true spinach, but it will withstand hot weather and continue on throughout the summer.

CHARD is either loved or hated and there is no in-between. It has the advantage of growing indefinitely on and on into the late fall and can be substituted for spinach in many recipes. Like all leafy vegetables it is best when picked young. It is easy to grow and is pest-free. One planting will go on forever as long as you keep picking the outside leaves. Buy one packet of *Fordhook Giant* or *Lucullus*.

The ONION family is large, with many kissin' cousins. I insist upon having Leeks, Shallots, and two varieties of onions. All of these go in at the same time as your root vegetables; that is, early. If you can find good healthy shallot and garlic plants in your local market, plant them. Otherwise send for them with your seed order. They will multiply, so you can start with six shallots and six garlic cloves. Take up what you want in the fall.

Leave the rest in the garden, and in the spring when the tops are showing green, dig up and separate all the little bulbs and replant them.

We buy onion sets and the amount is really up to you as to how many onions you are inclined to use. We buy two pounds, one of *Southport White Bunching* which makes excellent scallions, and one of *Yellow Sweet Spanish* to see us through the winter.

Leeks are difficult to raise from seed sown directly in the garden, so if you don't want to start them indoors, buy the seedlings locally. I put in two dozen and often use them wintered over.

RHUBARB is another strong like or dislike but it combines well with many fruits, so five of these perennial plants should be welcome in any garden. It does like cool weather and is one of your "Welcome Spring" plants, ready for early pulling the year after you put it in. *MacDonald* and *Victoria* are good strains. It is a handsome plant and deserves a place to show off its large, beautiful (but poisonous) leaves. Harvest only the stalk, please.

ASPARAGUS is faithful and forever—well, for at least fifteen years. It is a bit of effort to put in an asparagus bed, but to all asparagus lovers well worth it. As to how much to plant, if you are going to do it at all, I assume that as a family you like asparagus—love it. And you will want to eat it, after the second year, two or three times a week, hot or cold, raw and cooked. If these assumptions are correct, and if my estimate is modest, I would suggest planting between sixty and seventy roots for a family of four asparagus lovers. You can fit thirty-five roots in a 50-foot row. *Mary Washington Rust Resistant* roots are best.

The TURNIP family has two popular members, Rutabagas and Turnips. They are very much the same in taste and some families consider them a vital part of holiday dinners. They grow the same way as beets, with the rutabaga taking about a month longer than the turnip, which matures anywhere from fifty to sixty days. We plant one or the other, not both, in August. A fifteen-foot row is sufficient for our needs.

That takes care of your early planting and you will have a welcome respite for about five weeks until it is time to put in the rest of the vegetables. Don't rush the season because all vegetables need warm weather and even if the seeds are in the ground they will not move until the earth and atmosphere warm up to their liking. In fact, they might rot.

Every garden must have a New Business Plan. Pick out one or two new vegetables and take a family vote on them. It might be a carrot such as *Goldinhart* or a new lettuce called *Buttercrunch* or *Green Ice*. Who has the fun of naming all these vegetables—and so aptly, too? Buttercrunch is truly buttery to the touch as well as to the taste.

We included POPCORN on our new business list a few years ago, mainly to interest the children. We found it so successful that we've grown it every year since. The kernels are extremely white compared to the commercial variety and produce a snowy bowl of fluff when popped in our old-fashioned corn popper on our modern electric stove. But don't forget the magic of a fire with chestnuts and popcorn and marshmallows on a cold winter's night. We use lots of coarse salt and melted butter on the popcorn or else we make it into wonderful sticky popcorn balls, so reminiscent of my childhood. I'm sure that we never ate them all; the fun was in the making. And everyone should do a cranberry and popcorn Christmas tree for the birds just once while her children are young enough to enjoy it and old enough to help with the stringing. Prepare yourself for the inevitable time when the cover is taken off the popper too soon and there is a wild shower of flying white pellets all over the room.

BEANS are one of your best crops for succession planting, so you will want to keep careful note of just when to put in new rows.

We start with sixteen feet of Green beans and sixteen feet of Limas at first; then we add another sixteen feet of green in two weeks. By doing this all summer up until late in July, we are assured of the proper amount of beans to use in reasonable amounts. Don't forget, there are a lot of other vegetables coming through at the same time and much as you may love beans, you can eat just so many. Also, you don't want your family to get overdosed all at once.

There is one question which comes to mind when discussing types of beans, of which there are many. Are you a true lima

bean lover? Many people aren't. Limas are a bother to shell, and you may think that the frozen product isn't that bad. We happen to love fresh limas and wait for the succotash season with bated breath, so we always put in about sixteen feet of lima beans. You can plant either the large *Fordhook* or the baby *Thaxter;* they both take about two and a half months to mature. Figure back from your first frost if you wish more than one planting.

We prefer bush beans to pole beans, but that may be part of our New England heritage, and the *Kentucky Wonder* pole bean does do well in northern gardens too. *Topcrop, Tendercrop* and *Blue Lake* are all good varieties of green bean and Eastern *Butterwax* or *Brittlewax* are your yellow beans.

SQUASHES could take a whole garden to themselves, and will if you let them. The catalogs give us such a wide variety that it is hard to choose. We settle for three summer squashes: *Zucchini Elite, Seneca Prolific,* and the early *White Bush Scallop.* The Zucchini is a graceful long glossy green squash with myriad uses; Seneca Prolific is the yellow squash we think of as "summer" or "crookneck"; Bush Scallop is a fairly new variety also known as "Pattypan." It is thick, with a saucer shape and a deep scalloped edge, ivory in color. Actually its appearance would place its natural habitat as either the seashore or outer space, not your garden. One packet of each and one planting of five hills each is enough.

Winter squashes—and they are the true squash—tend to run free and they need a lot of room to roam. If you'll notice, we have them in a separate area with the cucumbers, corn, and pumpkins. We like *Waltham Butternut* and the *Table Queen* acorn. There is a lovely little squash called *Golden Nugget* that grows on bush vines and therefore takes up less space. The fruits are small in size and bright orange in color and fun to grow. Two hills of each kind should be enough.

In the same area as your squashes, you had better put your CUCUMBERS. They are all related anyhow. Cucumbers don't necessarily resemble each other in appearance; they come in all shapes and sizes, and you just pick what you think you'd like from the catalog description.

Some of the standards are *Gemini, Triumph,* and *Challenger* for slicing. These can also be pickled while they are small—an advantage if you want to try pickles but don't want to give up space for the special "picklers." There is also a new hybrid that has been developed for all those who find cucumbers indigestible—and that is quite a sizeable group, although I have included a recipe for this later on. The new hybrid is called, appropriately enough, *Burpless* and it is similar to the extremely long French cucumber in looks.

Plant four hills of cucumbers in May when the soil is warm and, if you want some for fall use and pickling, put in another planting four to five weeks later. They are all fairly fast growing—about two and a half months.

Another close relative in the vine patch is the MELON. Very often this fruit is foregone in a garden because of space problems. If you could try just one or two varieties, you would find it a very rewarding project if you live in a warm enough area. Vine-ripened melons are a beautiful treat for late summer eating. The reason for their extra sweetness when home-grown is that the sugar content of muskmelons actually decreases when they are picked green. They must stay on the vine to realize their full sweetness.

Hearts of Gold, Gold Star and *Supermarket* are good early types and *Crenshaw* is a lovely late melon. The early melons take about three months and the late varieties can take four to mature. Two hills will give you an adequate supply and you must eat them when ripe, for they are not good keepers.

We like big *Connecticut Field* PUMPKINS for fall decorating and jack o'lanterns, and the *Small Sugar* for pies and puddings. There is something very basic and ancestral about pumpkins, and to see them in the field when much of the garden has gone by gives one a good, albeit nostalgic, feeling about the rewards of gardening. And, of course, children love pumpkins.

CORN? It does take up room and many

gardeners will say, "Don't bother, you can buy it anywhere along the road in August." But it is one of those vegetables that should be rushed from picking to pot, and I would recommend at least trying it to see if you think your own corn is worth growing. The general rule for planting seems to be: put more seeds in as soon as the latest planted begin to show. For amount, figure two good ears to a stalk. We put in, for our first planting, eight 8-foot rows. There are so many varieties that it is difficult to recommend, but our personal choices are *Country Gentleman,* an old-fashioned all-white corn; a gold and white hybrid called *Honey And Cream* or *Butter And Sugar;* and the yellow *Golden Bantam* or *Seneca Chief.* You should ask around in your own area as to which varieties do best, but do plant a little of each.

There are pros and cons about CABBAGE, accepting the fact that you like it. The pros are that it is a good fall vegetable, it will withstand low temperatures, and it is a good producer. The cons say that it takes up valuable garden space and takes a long time to grow. This is where personal preference plays a large part in the planning of your own garden. Will you eat enough cabbage to make it worthwhile? Or will you just eat the red cabbage, or just the white? Or do you like the lovely, curly-leafed *Savoy* which is milder in flavor? If you are going to put seed directly in the ground for a late fall crop, try *Danish Ballhead, Red Rock* or *Ruby Ball Red* and *Savoy King* or *Chieftain.* To get the early crops, you should start seeds indoors or plant sets. For amounts, figure your plants to be two feet apart.

If you don't want to grow cabbage, then *do* grow BROCCOLI. It is a handsome plant to have in the garden, and most rewarding, because it produces well into the fall after the first frost. Keep cutting and it will keep growing and, believe me, it is not the same thick-stalked vegetable that we are used to in the winter. *Italian Green Sprouting* to us is the best, and you can start your seeds inside and transplant after the last frost or start them directly in the ground in late May to produce a fall crop. Or you can buy eight plants from your local nursery and have broccoli in six weeks.

Some say CELERY should not be undertaken by the home gardener. Others say try it, you may be successful. Celery does like rich soil and a lot of moisture. It also needs coolish nights. If you can provide these necessities, then give it a whirl. The big question with this vegetable seems to be blanching. I say yes, it is necessary to blanch so that the stalks are not tough and stringy. But blanching is not that difficult a proposition. When your celery gets tall, just lay light boards along either side, on an angle of an inverted V. This will cover the stalks sufficiently and will save you the work of hilling. *Pascal* and *Fordhook* are good growers, and a ten-foot row should be sufficient unless you are avid celery eaters. You don't need to wait for full maturity to pick this plant; the stalks can be used from the time the plants are half grown.

CAULIFLOWER is perhaps best left to the experts, or at least not to be tried by the beginning gardener. However, once you get yourself established and you know the ground rules, then try it, remembering that it is best grown as a fall crop. It needs a lot of moisture, and you *must* protect the heads from sun by tying the leaves up over them as soon as they start to form. As you can see, it takes a bit of fussing over, but if you want a challenge in the garden, put in some *Snowball* cauliflower. It takes about two months to mature and, if you're lucky, it might look just like the picture in the catalog. I would advise buying plants; then you will know exactly how much you are getting, how much room in the garden they take, and how much you will have to eat!

There are certain vegetables that are best purchased in plant form, unless you wish to start them indoors and transplant the seedlings when the time is right. The first of these is EGGPLANT. Six plants are enough for our family. We are average eaters of this handsome vegetable which is so aptly named *Black Beauty* or *Early Beauty*. If I were a painter, I would love this vegetable just for its color and form; but I deplore the

January

fact that the glossy purple skin disappears in cooking. We must love it for its flavor alone. When serving eggplant, I like to use a few small ones in a centerpiece to accent the vegetable's beauty.

PEPPERS are the perfect foil for eggplant, whether in the casserole or as a part of the centerpiece. They come in two varieties, sweet and hot, and the only rule of thumb is not to plant one near the other, as the hot is dominating and will take over completely. We buy six plants of the sweet pepper and two of the hot; and never the twain shall meet.

The third member of this culinary trio is TOMATOES and, after waiting nine months for a home-grown, vine-ripened tomato, it doesn't seem as though we ever get enough of the glorious fruit. So we plant a dozen plants and eat tomatoes for every meal in every fashion. It is definitely the all-American vegetable-fruit, number one in sales of plants and seeds. There seems to be a tomato to suit every whim or wish, in all sizes and colors—red, yellow, orange, pink, tiny, small, medium, large and super-large. Try some old favorites such as *Rutgers, Beefsteak,* or *Marglobe* and then put in a few new brands such as *Big Boy, Big Early Hybrid, Fireball* or *Harris Supersonic.* Do put in a couple of the small-fruited varieties either in the garden or on the terrace. You can have both yellow and red in the "cocktail" tomato.

Notwithstanding the cheerful look of your catalogs, January is a drear month and needs some cheer. It is a time for soup, and you can satisfy your creative ego by making it from vegetables that you have wintered over. Let's start with the leek, an unknown quantity to many cooks and gardeners in this country.

The leek is a member of the onion family, although milder and sweeter in flavor. You may have seen it pictured as the badge of the Welshman, a flat solid green leaf growing down into a cylindrical bulb. Leeks have been called "poor man's asparagus" but unless you grow them yourself you'll find them a "rich man's delicacy" in the markets. Luckily, they are easy to grow. Start them early in the spring and pay them no heed until fall when you can either dig them up or leave them in the ground mulched with hay over the winter.

In this way you can have leeks available all winter and on a cold snowy day make up a steaming pot of an aromatic French peasant concoction called Pistou Soup. Made with a beef or chicken stock base and containing various vegetables, it lends itself to the conditions of your pantry shelf at the moment, and you may suit yourself as to the contents, just being sure to include the final addition of garlic, oil, herbs, and egg yolk. With a simple omelet and dessert, you have a robust supper.

Soupe au Pistou

White part of two leeks, sliced
1 cup diced onion
1 tbsp. butter
1 tbsp. oil
1 cup green beans in 1-inch pieces
1 cup diced potatoes
1 cup canned Italian tomatoes
6 cups beef stock
½ cup vermicelli in 1-inch pieces
Salt and pepper

Cook leeks and onion in butter and oil until they are translucent. Add vegetables and stock. Cover and bring to a boil. Reduce heat and simmer for 30 minutes until vegetables are done. Add vermicelli after 15 minutes. Season with salt and pepper.

Mix together:

2 cloves garlic, crushed
½ tsp. dried basil
¼ tsp. dried thyme
¼ tsp. dried sage
2 egg yolks
¼ cup oil
½ cup grated Cheddar or Swiss cheese

Mash garlic with herbs. Stir in yolks with fork. Add oil slowly, stirring constantly. Put above mixture into soup tureen and add hot soup gradually, stirring to prevent curdling yolks. Sprinkle with cheese.

The password for leek is clean. Because they grow either in hills or in trenches, the dirt can go down deep into their many layers. Before cooking, you should cut off the white bulb with about an inch of green attached and soak it in cold water. If the leeks are extremely sandy, cut down lengthwise almost to the bottom and wash out with cold water or soak for half an hour. Now your leeks are ready for braising and, of course, you are going to save the green tops for flavoring the soup or stew pot. To braise leeks or celery: Place the vegetable in buttered shallow dish. Add a small amount of liquid, either water or stock, about halfway up vegetable. Cover tightly and simmer over low heat or place in a moderate oven until tender and easily pierced with a knife point. Check after fifteen minutes. Do not overcook. Remove vegetable. Reduce liquid somewhat and add butter. Pour over vegetable and serve. Or remove vegetable from liquid and serve cold with a vinaigrette sauce.

Because Monday is often referred to as "blue" and many have been heard to say that they wished the week could begin on Tuesday, it is a good idea to have an extra-special meal on Monday night. Save the weekend leftovers until Tuesday, or even Wednesday, when you feel more imaginative.

For an inspired Monday night dinner featuring the leek, which you have pulled from the frozen earth, there is a European dish somewhat mysteriously called Belgian Waterzooie. With the character of a souplike stew, it is a filling dish when served with good bread, some cheese and fruit. It is best served in a flat soup plate, and you should provide a knife as well as a soup spoon. The flavor is one of subtle lemon cream over chicken and its appearance is deceptively springlike.

Belgian Waterzooie

3 tbsp. butter
1 tbsp. oil
4 leeks, white parts chopped
4 celery stalks, chopped
3 carrots, chopped
1 onion, chopped
3 sprigs parsley

¼ tsp. thyme
1 bay leaf
2 2½-3 lb. chickens
6 cups chicken broth
3 egg yolks
½ cup heavy cream
   juice of 1 lemon
   salt and pepper

Cook vegetables and herbs in butter and oil until soft, not brown. Put this mixture into large casserole and place whole chickens on top. Pour in broth. Cover, bring to a boil, and simmer for one hour until chicken is tender. Remove chicken and cool. When cool enough to handle, remove skin and large bones, as many as possible. Keep chicken in fairly large pieces. Strain broth and reduce by boiling over high heat until you have approximately 4 cups. Beat together the yolks and cream. Slowly stir in broth and lemon juice, salt and pepper to taste. Place chicken pieces in soup tureen and pour sauce over. Sprinkle ¼ cup chopped parsley over top. It is customary to serve this dish with buttered brown bread.

Another interesting and somewhat different main dish for lunch or dinner is a leek and white wine quiche. It's interesting because we do not think of having pie as a main course and, in reality, a quiche is nothing more or less than a custard pie with various fillings. You can use any number of vegetables or vegetable and meat, chicken, or fish combinations and it may never be the same twice. If you are prone to winter picnics, you will fasten onto the quiche idea with enthusiasm because a quiche travels well and can, indeed should, be served at room temperature.

There is a basic technique that seems to work very well for all such custard pies. Remember that it takes two eggs to thicken one cup of milk. Fill your pie pan with a measuring cup of water to just under the rim to find out exactly how much liquid it will hold. Subtract the amount of solid filling you are using and there you have the amount of liquid mixture you will use for that particular quiche. With a salad or hot green vegetable and a fruit dessert (not pie, please) you have a good, substantial meal. A quiche can also be baked without its pastry shell and then it becomes a flan, which is nice for Sunday morning breakfast. If you bake two different kinds of flans or quiches and add fruit and coffee, you might as well ask the neighbors in for brunch. Include the children. This type of fare seems to appeal to them, probably because they never dreamed they would be allowed to have pie for breakfast. Of course, in Colonial times a fruit or custard pie was always included on the breakfast menu, and usually more than one kind.

Leek and White Wine Quiche

½ cup white part of leek, minced
½ cup dry white wine
 6 eggs
 3 cups medium cream
 1 tsp. salt
¼ tsp. white pepper or cayenne
     Nutmeg
12 oz. grated Swiss or Gruyère cheese
 1 10-inch pastry shell prebaked for 10 minutes

Place leeks and wine in pan and bring to a boil. Simmer for 2 minutes. Cool. Beat together the eggs, cream, seasonings and wine-leek mixture. Sprinkle cheese in pie shell. Pour custard in. Bake at 325° for 45-50 minutes until custard is firm. To test: insert knife at edge of pie. If it comes out clean, take pie out of oven. It will continue to cook in the pan. Let cool slightly before cutting.

Pity the parsnip; it is low man on the garden totem pole. Perhaps this is because, like most root vegetables, it was part of the pioneer's cellar, something that was eaten all year long because there just wasn't anything else. A truly unexciting vegetable. But now we labor much longer than our grandmothers to glamorize such root cellar staples.

Until I was on my own in the kitchen and somewhat more adventurous than a new bride will be, I never knew that there was such a thing as a parsnip. Now parsnips help to liven our winter menus. Like carrots, they are sweeter after the first frost, so leave them in the ground—even through the winter if you wish. It will give you a feeling of closeness to your pioneer ancestors to be digging your parsnips on a cold January day. Once the ground thaws, however, their sweetness disappears and they become bitter and more like the vegetable which Fanny Farmer described as "mostly cattle food."

Treat parsnips as you would a sweet potato, adding apples or onions, brown sugar and nutmeg or cinnamon to slices of cooked, peeled parsnips, and baking all together to amalgamate the flavors. Or mash them and add some of the natural juices of a roast, especially a pot roast which has been cooked in strong black coffee or a spicy combination of horseradish, cranberries and allspice. Working on the theory that practically everything lends itself to a soufflé, I discovered that parsnips do also. By adding a cup of puréed parsnip, well seasoned with salt, paprika, brown sugar, and a bit of dry mustard, you have a nice accompaniment to roast pork or chicken.

Parsnip Soufflé

     3 tbsp. butter
     3 tbsp. flour
 ½ cup chicken broth
 ½ cup milk
     1 cup puréed parsnip
     1 tsp. salt
 ½ tsp. paprika
     1 tbsp. brown sugar
     1 tsp. dry mustard
     5 egg yolks
     6 egg whites

Melt butter in saucepan over high heat. Stir in flour and cook, stirring until mixture, or roux, is golden and bubbly. This is important to cook the flour. Add liquids, all at once, and stir over heat until thick and smooth. Remove from heat. Season parsnip with salt, paprika, brown sugar, and mustard. Taste and season more highly if you wish. Remember that egg whites detract from the seasoning. Stir yolks into sauce mixture. Add parsnip and mix well. Beat whites until stiff with ½ tsp. salt. Fold into parsnip and yolk mixture. Pour into a 1½-quart soufflé dish. Bake at 325° for 25-30 minutes until firm. Serve immediately.

Obviously, parsnips need a lot of seasoning, but have I managed to glamorize this very mundane vegetable enough so that you'll include it in your garden—in spite of Fanny Farmer?

February

THIS IS the shortest month by count but many times the longest, as we wait for signs of spring. We may have more and more snow during these twenty-eight days, but the winter solstice is past, and the days are longer from dawn to dusk. The sunrises are bright and clear, and if you live on a hill you can go out early and see morning arriving on one side and night departing on the other. It is at moments like this that we understand the Greek feeling for giving names to the sun and the moon and the stars, for making gods of them and worshiping their power. It is an exhilarating time of day, and we feel very much attuned to Nature as we see the bare outlines of her world. We spend the long Sunday afternoons making diagrams for the garden and studying the seed catalogs which continue to come in.

One of the most rewarding planting projects we ever embarked upon was putting in of a small orchard. This is a good time to consider such an idea in your overall garden plan. It's nice to have a continuity to your food growing area if possible, but if you have any kind of a hill on your property, that is the ideal spot for an orchard. Fruit trees like being up and away from pockets of frost, and that is the reason many commercial orchards are placed high on windy hills.

We have come up with a planting plan that is not only fun but feasible for any size lot. Every bush or tree or shrub or vine that we plant bears edible fruit. Ideally, we would like to have hedges of blueberry and blackberry, a driveway lined with fruit trees, a grove of nut trees, a grape arbor (with a white iron bench under it), and a raspberry patch near enough to the kitchen door to gather them easily for breakfast. Once upon a time we optimistically thought that there would be enough for the birds and ourselves. Not so. The birds are greedier and quicker than we, so now we net our cherry trees and blueberry bushes.

Our trees are dwarf, planted ten feet apart, and in the spring they make a fairyland of blossoms as each in its turn presents a floral display that is hard to equal.

One of the many reasons for planting an orchard is the great satisfaction of producing your own fruit, eating it ripe from the tree

nostalgic yen for, or brand-new varieties that have been developed by a state testing station and are not yet on the market. We Americans seem to be so conditioned to McIntosh and Delicious that we don't think of any other kinds of apples. Yet we can plant and have our own *Poundsweet, Sheepnose,* or *Spitzenbergs* (Thomas Jefferson's favorite apple). The white *Belle of Georgia* peach has a flavor and sweetness that defies description. And who has seen pie cherries in the supermarkets lately?

Here are some suggestions for a small family-sized orchard: Sixteen fruit trees is a good number for a small orchard. We put in the dwarf size and found that they grew very rapidly. We started with two-year trees partly branched, although you could put in one-year whips. They actually don't take that long to catch up to the others.

Six APPLE trees seemed a good number with early fall and late fall ripening. *Winesap* is my favorite for an all-purpose apple that comes in late fall. I also like the *Macoun* which is similar to the McIntosh but ripens later. *Wealthy* is a nice, old-fashioned early

and preserving the surplus in conserves, jam, jellies, sauces, or that wonderful old-fashioned mixture called *Tutti-Frutti* or *Rum Pot.*

Another sound reason for growing your own fruit is being able to have types that are not available commercially. These may be kinds that you knew as a child and have a

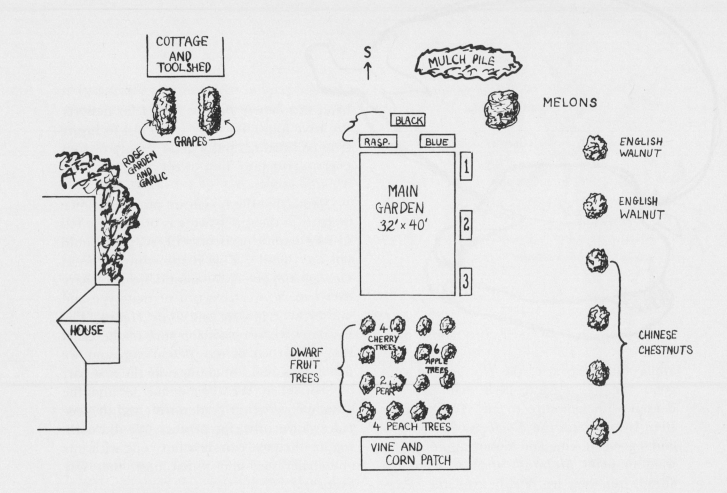

COTTAGE AND TOOLSHED

GRAPES

S ↑

MULCH PILE

MELONS

ROSE GARDEN AND GARLIC

BLACK

RASP.   BLUE

1

MAIN GARDEN 32' x 40'

2

3

ENGLISH WALNUT

ENGLISH WALNUT

HOUSE

DWARF FRUIT TREES

4 CHERRY TREES

6 APPLE TREES

2 PEAR

4 PEACH TREES

VINE AND CORN PATCH

CHINESE CHESTNUTS

1. RHUBARB, JERUSALEM ART., HOT PEPPERS
2. STRAWBERRIES
3. ASPARAGUS

↓ N

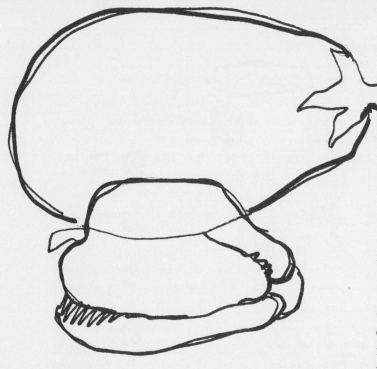

apple and, of course, the *Cortland* is very good and has a white flesh that does not darken with exposure to air. The *Gravenstein* is early and the *Northern Spy* is later and a good cooking and dessert apple. If you want to plant *McIntosh* and *Delicious*, go ahead, but they are readily available everywhere.

PEAR trees are lovely to look at in the spring and it is worth putting in two kinds, a *Bartlett* which is so good for eating out of hand and *Beurre Bosc* or *Seckel* for desserts. We have four CHERRY trees, just to insure cross-pollination, and a good supply of sour cherries for pie. Two sweet *Bing* and two *Montmorency* tart.

I think that the reason we put in our own orchard in the first place was because we fell in love with a particular PEACH we could not buy locally. This is the white *Belle of Georgia* and one of the most delicious I have ever had. So we have two of that type and one each of *Elberta* and *Hale Haven*. The first year we were not too sure of the exact time of arrival of our peach crop and we made the mistake of going away the first part of September. We came home to find the ground covered with fallen fruit and the tree laden down with ripe peaches. We did nothing for the next two days but cope with our abundant crop, and it has been that way every year.

RASPBERRIES are rewarding and they require little care except for pruning out the dead canes in the winter and cutting down all the canes that have borne fruit after they are through bearing. The don't need fertilizing—just a lot of good hot sun and good drainage. We put in two dozen plants. Our first crop appears in July, and if we're lucky there's a short second crop in the fall. *Indian Summer* is the earliest to ripen and will produce two crops. *Latham* and *Newburgh* are for mid-season enjoyment.

The BLACKBERRY could make its own completely impenetrable hedge, I am sure, because it is the one fruit that requires gloves for pruning. There is a new *Thornfree* blackberry, but we have the *Darrow* variety which produces big, fat berries every year in early July. A small patch of six plants is sufficient for our needs.

We do use BLUEBERRIES and I wish that we had room for more than six plants, but one must stop somewhere, although a berry hedgerow is most appealing. There are many kinds of blueberries and new ones are being developed all the time. Just be sure to plant at least two different varieties for cross-pollination. Perhaps the easiest way would be to order a "collection" which will include at least six different kinds.

GRAPES are beautiful, right from the spring, when their silvery leaves first appear, to fall when clusters of purple and white fruit hang heavily from the arbor. Esthetically they are an addition to any property, and the juice, jam and jelly they produce is part of our breakfast fare all winter long. Choose *Concord,* of course, for its beautiful color if nothing else, although this grape makes one of the best and most unusual pies I have ever had. You can buy wine varieties, but we prefer the table and dessert grapes. Eight vines on an arbor are perfect and for color contrast you could plant an early black *Fredonia,* an early red *Delaware,* a mid-sea-

son white *Niagara,* a late red *Catawba* and a late *Golden Muscat.*

It is hard to resist STRAWBERRIES. They are part of the romance of June and one perfect strawberry shortcake is worth the whole strawberry bed. The best catalog will give you a wide variety of choices with accurate information as to which is early, mid-season, or late, and what is the best use for each type. I suggest starting with twenty-five plants and adding more each year.

This month you must really get down to business and make a garden plan to fit in all those things I've discussed that you'll want. Think big, but start small. Nature, being dependable in the long run, will always provide another gardening season, and it is too bad to discourage yourself the first year with too large an area to work easily.

After years of coping in the garden with vines that crawled all over the tomatoes, peppers and beans, we have relegated the vine vegetable to the outer edge. A 32 by 8-foot area takes care of cucumbers, melons, winter squashes and pumpkins along with the corn, and they can happily intertwine around each other. As one fanciful child said, "That part of the garden looks as if it were waiting to grab anyone who came near it." But it is a

system that worked very well for the Indians, and they also had a method of fertilization that worked very well: burying fish heads in the corn hills. We cannot do that, practically speaking, but there is on the market a natural fish emulsion fertilizer which seems to do wonders. We sprinkle it on when the plants are young, and perhaps it's the odor that makes them spring up away from the ground, but they certainly do make rapid progress.

For the something new in your garden, try just a small amount at first. Talk shop with other gardeners as to what does well in your area, or ask your county extension agent for advice. Seek out the old-timers living around you. Some of them are wonderful gardeners and full of information that you could never get anywhere else.

We have a neighbor who has moved here recently from California, and she is determined to try globe artichokes. We are greatly interested in her project, though the globe artichoke has certainly never been considered a Connecticut crop. Not so, however, another ARTICHOKE called *Jerusalem*. This fascinating tuber grows like a sunflower. As

a matter of fact, it *is* related to the sunflower. As someone said, it thrives in the garden of neglect, and once it gets going it is almost impossible to stop. So beware where you plant it. You can order the tubers from certain seed houses or you may see them in your market. Plant them three to four inches down in the earth, remembering that they will probably grow to eight feet in height. A large yellow flower appears in August. The artichoke tubers can be harvested in the fall or left in the ground and dug out during the winter as you need them. Each tuber you plant will multiply into several more.

Aside from its curiosity value, does this Jerusalem artichoke do anything for us in the culinary department? It certainly does and it is fun to have a different vegetable to play with. I cannot say "new" but rather a revival of an old vegetable with some new cooking possibilities. The old-fashioned way of using this tuber was simply to boil it and mash it with potatoes—good but not very imaginative. It has a crisp texture similar to that of a water chestnut or radish. Its flavor is a bit nutty but not strong. I think that it is easier to peel the artichoke when raw (and it is very good sliced into a salad just this way). If you wish to peel and parboil the artichokes in boiling salted water for five minutes, then they are ready to be added to a chicken pot pie or a lamb or beef stew (the latter shortly before serving). They are also good served with cream or in a vinaigrette sauce. We'll talk about Jerusalem artichokes later, in the fall, but here's one recipe now:

Artichoke pickle is a common relish on Southern dinner tables since the vegetable grows wild in the fields and by the roadside, and if you do plant your own Jerusalem artichokes, it is a very worthwhile way to preserve some of your crop. Made with red peppers, it is a pretty condiment and makes an unusual and much appreciated gift.

Jerusalem Artichoke Pickle

1 qt. Jerusalem artichokes
3 tbsp. salt
1 qt. onions
1 pt. red bell peppers
1 qt. vinegar
2 cups sugar
1 tsp. celery seed
½ tsp. red pepper
3 tsp. mustard seed
1 tbsp. turmeric
2 tbsp. dry mustard

Peel and grind artichokes. Sprinkle salt over artichokes and let stand 1 hour. Pour off liquid. Grind onions and peppers. Combine all ingredients and bring to a boil. Boil for 10 minutes. Seal in jars.

Farming today can be accomplished much more easily than in our grandfathers' time with its limited machinery and technical knowledge. However, in talking to real dirt farmers you may find they still pay heed to some of the things their grandfathers taught them. Symbiosis, or companion planting, is old-fashioned but it works. Plant garlic near your roses and it will keep away the aphids. Potatoes with the beans prevents Mexican bean beetle, although there is the possibility that you may attract the potato beetle. To combat all of this you can plant marigolds and nasturtiums in the immediate area. As a matter of fact, it is a cheerful note to include some flowers in your vegetable garden, and they usually do very well there.

Since the method is as old as the Indians, it stands to reason that the beans-corn-squash combination is one that works. Planted together, they give nourishment to each other and also take up less space, since the squash can crawl along the ground under the other two erect plants.

HERBS have always been cited for their mysterious powers—from love potions to fever reducers—so we may as well plant dill with the tomatoes and thyme with the broccoli to lure away the worms. Actually dill grows best in the vegetable garden anyhow because it likes heavier fertilization and should be planted in fairly sizeable clumps. It is not a plant that likes to stand alone but needs to lean on others for support.

It is interesting that some companionable combinations are just as good on the dinner plate as in the garden: carrots and peas, onions and beans, radishes and lettuce, cucum-bers and beans. Barely-cooked tiny green beans and raw cucumbers diced, both marinated together in a simple French dressing, make a good mid-summer salad. Perhaps we should just relax and let nature lead the way.

It is both the weakness and the strength of the gardener that he gets carried away by the end result and tends to make light of the toil of preparation. Weakness because his dreams tend to outweigh his capacities; strength because there is truth in the old adage about dangling carrots in front of a horse's nose to spur his progress.

But back to basics: Soil preparation *is* important and is not overrated. Just digging a patch and putting in a few seeds will not produce much that is edible. With our present garden, we covered the area with hay and let it lie fallow for a year, thereby killing grass and weeds and enriching the soil all in one process. Circumstances dictated this approach, as a vegetable garden was not feasible that year. If we had wanted to start right in, we would have pitchforked, roto-tilled, fertilized, and raked, raked, raked until we had a rich brown patch of earth, bordered by boards or bricks to keep the weeds at bay and, eventually, some kind of fencing to do the same for the stray animals. A very attractive kind of edging, the type you will see at Mt. Vernon, for instance, is made of fruit trees espaliered on a split-rail fence—another way of getting your orchard without taking up too much space.

Location is important, because your vegetables hopefully will do well with a lot of sun and good drainage. In one record rainfall year many gardens literally held water because there was no place for it to go. After the soil finally dried out, the gardens had to be completely replanted. This comes under the heading of a gardener's lot; but there was a happy ending. The second crop did fine.

One top crop that you may still have in your garden in February is SWISS CHARD or KALE, and if you wondered last year why you planted it, now you know. They are beautiful leafy green vegetables, to be fully appreciated at this time of year. Actually chard is the oldest form of beet, although we treat the leaves like spinach, the stalk like

celery or asparagus, and ignore the root completely. How's that for a versatile vegetable with a split personality?

Milder in flavor than spinach, the leaves and stems are good raw in salads. To serve it cooked, you cut the stalks into one-inch pieces and cook them in boiling salted water for five minutes. Then add the torn leaves and cook until tender, about five minutes. Drain thoroughly and serve with butter, salt and pepper and nutmeg. Or fold the chard into a cheese-flavored cream sauce.

Of course, chard can be used as you would use spinach, in a soufflé or a ring mold with creamed mushrooms in the center. The one thing to remember in making a ring mold of a vegetable is to butter your mold very well. Otherwise you will have to do a massive patching job before you serve it, or turn the whole thing into a casserole with the creamed mushrooms covering all.

You undoubtedly have some CARROTS around in the garden somewhere. We all plant too many and, if it will make us feel any thriftier, we can say that we purposely left some in the ground to take care of our winter needs. It is probably better winter storage than we can provide today with our overheated houses and no real root cellars, though it really would not be difficult to build an old-fashioned root cellar (and we could use it for wine as well). But that is one of those projects that makes for good conversation in the winter and too much labor in the summer.

Our winter meals certainly need the color that carrots can offer. Just a few glazed carrots as an accent on the plate, or grated carrot in a corn or rice ring can paint a pretty picture, and if you get a bit discouraged by the carrot's size or shape, try some recipes that use it chopped, ground, or grated. On a particularly gray day you could amuse yourself by making an updated version of an old (1747) recipe called carrot pudding. It has a sweetness that is not unlike pecan pie and, with a little vanilla ice cream on top, is surprisingly delicious and appealing to children.

Carrot Tart

1 tart shell, pre-baked 10 minutes
½ cup finely grated carrot
½ cup finely chopped walnuts
2 whole eggs
1 egg yolk
½ cup + 2 tbsp. medium cream
6 tbsp. melted butter
3 tbsp. cognac
2 tbsp. orange liqueur or orange juice
6 tbsp. sugar
1 tsp. grated nutmeg

Beat filling ingredients together in order given with whisk or spoon. Pour into tart shell. Bake at 350° for 25 minutes. Tart is done when knife inserted into edge of filling comes out clean. Let cool slightly before cutting.

We shall return to carrots on the menu again when they actually are in the ground and growing.

We leave February with the vegetable seed order placed in the mailbox to the very faint sounds of the hounds of spring following on winter's traces.

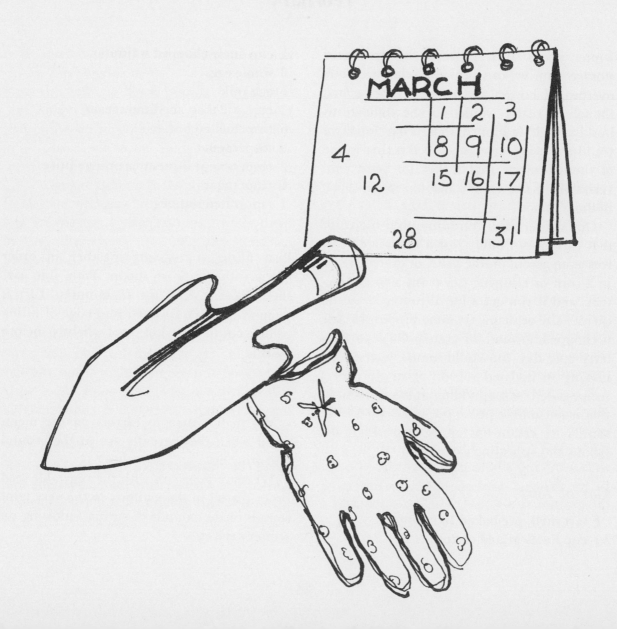

March

I HAVE planted my peas on the traditional seventeenth of March in a 22-degree temperature (granted that sometime earlier we had enough of a thaw to let me dig a shallow furrow in the ground). I have also planted them on that same date in sixty degrees, with the fair, soft breezes stirring. But no matter the temperature, when a gardener wakes up on March first, at least in our area, he can say to himself, "This is the month we should plant the peas," and his spring is about to begin.

Spring is as unpredictable as a young man's fancy, and we must doggedly keep in mind that Nature has not failed us yet with her inexorable cycle of change. And as surely as we plant those seeds, they *will* come up in their allotted time, no matter what.

It is perfectly possible to plant peas in March, depending on your climate and the severity of your winter, unless you are starting a new garden. Then you may have to wait until the whole garden is turned over. In an existing garden, however, providing the ground is not rock hard, you should be able to trace a furrow a half inch deep, drop in your peas, cover them snugly, and let nature take its course. Some say that this early planting makes no difference. Perhaps not, but there is a good feeling in knowing that, as the March winds harass the earth, there is something already on its way to the maturity that the warmth of summer brings.

This, of course, is the constant miracle of birth that makes gardening and growing and working with the soil so rewarding. And there is always a second chance. One year we lost our entire first crop of beans and zucchini due to excessive rainfall but we replanted and it all came up as planned.

Your seeds will be arriving probably on the coldest day of March, but take heart; you can always start some indoors, and the day will soon come when the wind blows without a bite and the time has come to DIG. While you're out with fork and rake, give some thought to the magic of herbs. They could be incorporated into the vegetable garden or, with a little more thought and planning (and digging), they could have a very decorative home of their own.

I have had various herb gardens, from kitchen door patches to perfectly planned patterns, and I finally have what for me is the most practical kind. It is a circle five feet in diameter, bordered by two rows of bricks and set in a sunny spot off the terrace where at the same time it is decorative and accessible. The kitchen door idea is fine if your kitchen is on the sunny side of the house. Mine isn't. If you have any interest in landscape design, or if you've always had a secret desire to try this kind of planning, now is your chance. You can spend hours in the local library studying plans of old-fashioned herb gardens and even find it necessary to take field trips to historic re-creations such as Sturbridge Village or Williamsburg or walk through the gardens at Mount Vernon, Monticello, or The Cloisters. The whole subject of herb garden design is fascinating, as is the lore of herbs, both medicinal and culinary.

I have confined my herbs to the culinary variety, and my five-foot garden holds the ten herbs that I actually use in cooking: chives, parsley, tarragon, thyme, rosemary, lemon balm, oregano, marjoram, sage, and basil—lots of basil! A larger herb garden you can fill very easily, but I want to control my gardens, not have them control me. So, as the vegetable garden increases in size, other things decrease a bit.

There is a special significance to the month of March that many of us are not aware of. It is the month of the "maple moon", and for those who live above the frost line, it means tapping the sugar maples for their precious sap which will eventually become maple syrup. Like our Jerusalem artichokes and our corn, maple syrup is a strictly American product.

The exact time for sugaring off is determined by the pulse of spring: when it thaws during the day and freezes at night. If you live in maple sugar country, just notice the tin pails hanging on the sugar maple trees. Then go home and just for fun tap your own. Everyone should try it once, remembering that it takes approximately forty gallons of sap to yield one of syrup. And also remember not to do your boiling-down inside the house. The steam created is enough to take down wallpaper.

The taste of maple seem to be born into most of us in North America. Many of our European friends do not like it; too sweet, they say. And the sight of blueberry pancakes in a golden pool of butter and syrup as a breakfast treat leaves them appalled. No matter. With maple syrup becoming scarcer and more expensive, it's one thing we will gladly keep to ourselves.

We will use it on baked bananas combined with lemon juice, cinnamon and ginger for an accompaniment to ham at the brunch or lunch table; or we might add a little brandy and slivered almonds and serve the bananas for dessert. We will make a rich, creamy maple nut mousse for a party, or a maple pecan cake for tea, or a maple coffee cake for breakfast. Or we could try a fall or winter casserole of apples and cooked sweet potatoes layered in a baking dish with butter, salt, pepper, nutmeg and maple syrup. And if your recipe calls for maple sugar, don't go out hunting for little maple cakes or figures packed in gift boxes; just boil some syrup down in a saucepan until it reaches the grainy stage and a candy thermometer registers 230°. Cool it slightly and beat with a wooden spoon until it is sugary.

Maple Nut Mousse

4 eggs, separated
1 cup maple syrup
1 tbsp. rum
2 cups heavy cream, whipped
1 cup walnuts, grated or chopped very fine

Cook egg yolks and maple syrup in double boiler over hot water until thick. Cool slightly. Add rum. Whip whites until stiff. Fold into syrup mixture. Fold in whipped cream. Sprinkle nuts into mold. Add 1/3 of mousse. Sprinkle more nuts, add mousse, more nuts, rest of mousse. Cover tightly and freeze for several hours.

Maple Bourbon Cake

　2　cups flour
　1　stick butter
½　cup sugar
　2　eggs
½　cup maple syrup
½　cup bourbon whiskey
2½ tsp. baking powder
½　tsp. salt
1½ cups pecans, coarsely chopped
½　tsp. nutmeg

Cream together the butter and sugar until smooth. Add eggs, one at a time, beating well. Mix baking powder, salt and nutmeg with flour and add alternately with maple syrup and bourbon. Stir in pecans. Pour into small greased tube pan or small loaf pan. Bake at 350° for 45-50 minutes. Sprinkle with powdered sugar when cool.

If you are a maple aficionado, you are already convinced that the best sauce in the world for ice cream is maple syrup boiled down until quite thick (take care it doesn't scorch) with a lot of chopped walnuts added. And with an obeisance to our Colonial ancestors, we can, in all honesty, add a tot of rum to this already devastating dessert. March might not be such a bad month after all.

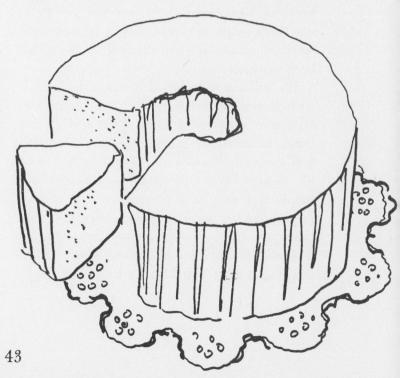

APRIL

April

Noted by poets and lyricists for its changeable ways, April surely can be the "cruelest month." Cruel in a very practical sense because now we feel a sense of urgency about our planting. Peas and lettuce love cool nights, so planting early is the theme song for early enjoyment of young and tender leaves of Romaine, Buttercrunch, Oakleaf and Salad Bowl. If April is as fickle as it is reputed to be, we gardeners may do a lot of our planting in the wind and the rain, but brave it out. The rewards are there.

Turn over as much soil as you will need for peas, carrots, lettuces, radishes, spinach, chard, beets, parsnips and onion sets. You are about to realize the dream you have been nurturing since the catalogs arrived. Turn in fertilizer and rake it all well.

I used to be guided by impulse and tended to be somewhat haphazard in the planting, but my methodical husband has finally persuaded me that the best line is a straight one, and we mark our rows carefully with string and sticks. You can plant rows a lot closer than you think; just leave a ten-inch foot-path in between and don't forget about your companion planting. Plant one more row of peas the second week in April.

All root vegetables go in now, although you will be doing successive planting on carrots and beets, so don't overdo it the first time. Neither of these vegetables freezes very well, so you don't want an over-abundance early in the season. Drop a few radish seeds along the carrot row. They will mark the row and help break the ground for that graceful green top that is so seldom seen in a market these days. That is just one more reason to grow your own. Don't forget the esthetic side of gardening.

Carrot seeds are so tiny, the plantlets are bound to need thinning and transplanting. When they get to that point, take a pencil to the garden with you. Poke a hole in the ground and carefully insert the spindly orange root. This will insure getting nice straight carrots rather than gnarled, twisted ones. It is also a much easier way of getting those tiny wisps into the ground.

Lettuce seeds are also hard to control. It is

THE BLANCHARD'S GARDEN IS 32' × 40'
(dates shown are for Connecticut plantings)

TOMATOES

BROCCOLI

CABBAGE

PEPPERS (SWEET)   EGG PLANTS

⊗ RADISHES $6/1$

SNAP GREEN BEANS $5/1$ ⊗ ... $5/15$

FORD HOOK LIMAS $6/1$ | SNAP GREEN BEANS $6/1$

⊗ OAK LEAF $4/1$ | ⊗ COS $4/1$ | ⊗ BUTTERCRUNCH $4/1$

ZUCCHINI $6/1$ PATTY PAN $6/1$ YELLOW CROOK NECK $6/1$

⊗ BEETS $4/1$ | ⊗ CARROTS $4/1$

⊗ BIBB $4/1$ | ⊗ BOSTON $4/1$ | ⊗ COS $5/1$

SPINACH $4/1 + 8/15$ | CHARD $6/15$

ONIONS $6/1$ — LEEK SETS $5/1$

SHALLOT SETS $5/15$

PARSNIPS $6/1$ | TURNIPS $6/1$

⊗ PEAS $3/17$

⊗ PEAS $4/15$

POTATOES $6/1$

RADISHES $4/1$ | RADISHES $5/1$

⊗ SUCCESSION PLANTINGS

47

a lovely idea to think that if you plant v-e-r-y carefully, you won't have to thin, but that's just not so. I wait until the plants are a decent size, however, and then transplant them into another part of my garden or give some to a neighbor. By then you can eat a great deal of what you thin. Thinning passes for work but can be a very pleasant pastime if you choose a nice warm day and just sit on the hay mulch and thin without thinking, letting Nature's sounds carry you out of the world for an hour or so.

Plant some parsley now and scatter English cress seeds around the empty spaces in your herb garden to fill it up. This cress grows fast and has a delightful peppery flavor in salads or sandwiches. You might want to try two kinds of parsley, the curly-leafed and the smooth-leafed. The curly is best for garnish and fried parsley, if you like that sort of thing, while the flat has a stronger flavor. An interesting fact about parsley is that much of the flavor is in the stems, so always include a bit of stem when chopping it for a recipe.

The grass grows, the leaf buds burgeon and the dandelion crop appears larger than last year's. Described as refreshingly bitter, DANDELIONS are a welcome spring tonic and a fresh green to include in tired salads. It is interesting to note that so many of our early spring greens have a definitely bitter taste, as if nature knew what our bodies needed after the long winter's nap.

To avoid an unpleasant flavor to your dandelion greens, pick them young before the flowers blossom, and if possible get them from a field rather than your own lawn. If you are initiating your family into the practice of trying wild greens, start slowly with a few leaves or some tender roots, tossed with the usual lettuce salad. Or you may make the following dressing, an old Pennsylvania Dutch recipe which is delicious on any greens.

April

Bibs Brown's Dressing for Dandelions

Cut 4 slices bacon into small pieces and fry. Pour off all but 3 tbsp. fat. When bacon is crisp, add 1 heaping tsp. flour and stir smooth. Brown this mixture. In a bowl crack 2 eggs and beat just enough to break yolks. Add about ½ tsp. salt and about ¾ cup brown sugar and ¾ cup vinegar. Add 2 tbsp. milk or cream. Mix all together and pour into bacon batter and cook. If you are using this on lettuce, add 1 heaping tsp. mustard. Add two chopped hard-cooked eggs. Pour over salad greens. Taste before adding mixture to bacon. Add more sugar or vinegar if necessary.

The strongest medicine of all made from dandelions is boiled greens with a piece of salt pork in the pot. It is really the old New England "mess of greens," and unless you really like such things, it is just that. The bitterness can be solved, though, if you change the water several times during the cooking.

This does seem to be the time of year when we want freshness in our meals. There is a temptation to buy more tomatoes, even though we know that they will taste no better than they did last winter and we really should wait for the natives. Ah, but it is such a long wait! But with some watercress leaves, snips off your garlic plants, dandelion greens and milkweed shoots, and the delicate fiddlehead fern, so highly prized by those who really know their wild greens, all tossed in small quantities into store-bought lettuce, you have a true tonic of a salad.

WATERCRESS by the bubbling brook is another sign of spring and anyone who has a brook should certainly plant some. Its faintly bitter, pungent flavor reminds us of its healthful properties—lots of iron—and enhances the delicacy of a wonderful soup. Watercress is a handsome garnish for roast chicken or meats which tend to look a bit naked on their platters. If you have to garnish and then refrigerate, just sprinkle a bit of oil on the leaves; it keeps them fresh. Also, just the leaves for garnish tends to give the effect of a lot of grass clippings. Always use the stems for character.

If it is still a sign of good manners that the guests should observe and follow their hostess, then set a good example by eating your watercress. It is a shame to send it to the compost heap. Cress doubles its role when it is used as a bed for fish fillets or steaks. It holds moisture and acts as decoration at the same time.

Watercress Cream

1 bunch watercress leaves
3 cups chicken broth
4 tbsp. butter
⅓ cup cream
3 tbsp. flour
1 cup milk
½ tsp. salt
   pepper
¼ tsp. nutmeg

Chop cress fine. Put in saucepan with broth and bring to boil. Simmer for 20 minutes. Make a roux of flour and butter, cooking until smooth and bubbly. Stir in milk and cook until smooth. Add this mixture to watercress and stock and simmer until thick. Add cream and seasonings. Serve hot or cold.

Green Baked Fish

1 lb. haddock
4 ripe tomato slices ½-inch thick
1 bunch watercress
1 tbsp. minced shallot
¼ cup oil
2 tbsp. flour
1 tsp. sugar
   paprika, salt and pepper

Make a thick bed of watercress with stems on bottom of greased shallow baking dish. Place fish on top. Cover with tomato slices. Sprinkle with shallots. Mix oil with flour and seasonings. Beat together with fork. Pour over fish. Bake at 350° for 20-30 minutes.

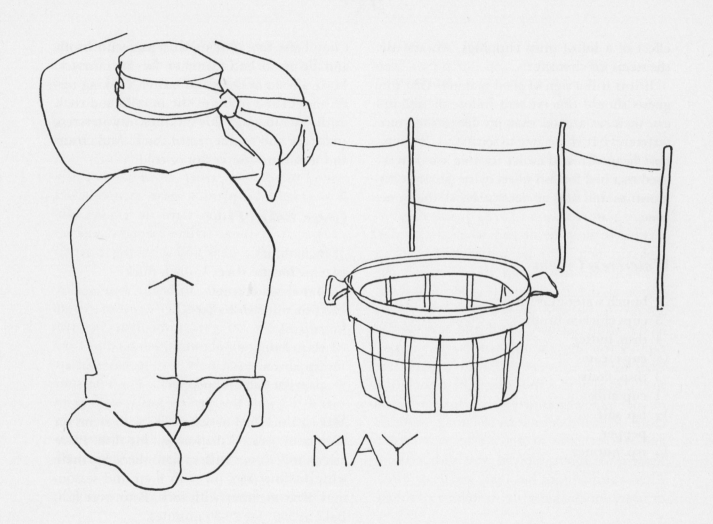

MAY

May

As APRIL steps softly into May, we feel the greening all around us, and our pulses keep time with Nature as the buds unfold. The daffodils are the harbingers of spring, and the willows are the first to bear new green leaves. The whole world seems full of scent and blossom, and each morning we inspect the trees and bushes to see what progress has been made. But no matter how closely we watch, Nature always takes us by surprise.

This is the time of year when the garden looks its best. Around it the orchard is in blossom; the lilacs scent the clear air; the dogwoods are in full flower—and there is not a weed to be seen, as yet. Peas are coming along, while lettuce, chard and spinach are rapidly reaching the thinning stage, and radishes are ready for eating. May is a good time in the garden and should see the completion of your planting efforts except for succession crops. Replant short rows of lettuce, radishes and carrots early in May. The peas need a fence just about now, if you didn't do it when you planted. Put up a length of three- or four-foot chicken wire stretching from one end of the row to the other, right down the middle of the pea plants so they can cling to both sides. The broccoli and cabbage can go in about the middle of the month or earlier. Around Memorial Day will be the time to plant the last of your garden, and time enough to get in the other herbs.

As I mentioned earlier, sweet and hot peppers cannot be planted near each other. I have a small isolation ward for garden outcasts such as these Italian peppers and for Jerusalem artichokes and anything I'm trying for the first time.

May is not too soon to begin your mulching, the carefree gardener's manna from heaven. As in all gardening there are two schools of thought about mulching, but from my experience the only way to have an enjoyable summer is to mulch. The one summer I did not, the garden was a disaster by the end of July with weeds as high as the elephant's eye. We use hay, but grass clippings, leaves, buckwheat hulls or cocoa shells are all satisfactory.

There are various reasons for mulching. It

does keep weeds down to a minimum. It does keep moisture in the ground and in a drought year this is very important (but be careful of it in a very wet year). And it does put nourishment back into the soil. One thing gardening teaches us is give and take —such a basic principle that we tend to forget it. What we take out of the soil we must eventually put back, and the more we put in, the better our crops will be.

Hay mulch should be laid down between the rows as soon as your plantings start to come through the ground. We put it about a foot deep. That seems like a lot of hay but we have some pretty tough weeds to combat. In our 32 by 40-foot garden we use about twenty bales of hay. It is worth it.

ASPARAGUS

It has been said that if one listens closely, one can hear the asparagus growing, and who am I to dispute such a fanciful tale? I would like to believe it. One day we see an inch of purple top showing. Two days later we pick enough to fill an omelet. And soon there is enough for the first real meal, with the name "Spring" on it: asparagus with lemon butter, leg of spring lamb, potatoes with chives, and a fresh rhubarb pie.

The cooking of asparagus seems to be a controversial matter. I have tried various ways, all designed to produce spears that are crisp, top and bottom. If you are picking from your own bed, use one of two methods. Either cut the spears with a knife just below the surface or go through the garden and break off the tender tops. Peel the stems with a vegetable peeler almost up to the heads. The basic idea is to keep the whole stalk at an even crispness, so peel off the tough outer skin on the bottom.

Like many vegetables, asparagus should be cooked just before eating. A long wait makes it limp. My favorite method is to lay the spears in a large skillet. Pour in cold water about halfway up to the spears. Salt. Cover the pan and put over high heat. Test for doneness in five minutes by inserting the point of a knife into the fattest spear. Depending on the thickness of the stems, the asparagus should be tender-crisp in seven to ten minutes. Drain and dry on paper towels.

Now as to the eating of asparagus—or perhaps you didn't realize that this also could be a subject for controversy. In the United States we eat our asparagus with a knife and fork. In its European birthplace it is eaten with the fingers. Therefore, the spears cannot be limp like spaghetti. They must be firm enough to dip into a sauce, either butter and lemon or butter and egg. Actually it is considered bad manners to use a knife and fork for asparagus in Europe. Using the fingers is considered poor manners here, but we can borrow the idea of cooking this vegetable to a firm, not limp, stage. We also can borrow some of their sauces, which are varied and delicious.

May

Maltese Sauce

3½ tbsp. white vinegar
2½ tbsp. water
   freshly ground pepper
 3 large egg yolks
 1 stick butter
   juice and grated rind of 1 orange
   salt to taste
 ½ tsp. lemon juice

Boil vinegar, water, and pepper in small saucepan until they are reduced to 1 tbsp. Put yolks in small heavy saucepan with butter which has been cut into 8 pieces. Put saucepan on asbestos pad over low heat. Stir yolks and butter together until butter melts. Mixture will thicken. Add vinegar, orange juice and rind, salt and lemon juice. Whisk all together. Leave until ready to serve. If mixture should curdle because heat is too high, whisk in an ice cube, beating until mixture becomes smooth.

Hollandaise Sauce

3 large egg yolks
1 stick butter
  salt to taste
1 tbsp. lemon juice
  white pepper

Put yolks and cut up stick of butter into saucepan and proceed as in above recipe. Add lemon juice and seasonings to taste.

Belgian Asparagus

1½ lbs. asparagus
 ½ cup sour cream
   toasted bread crumbs
   melted butter

Cook asparagus as in basic recipe. Drain and dry. Place in buttered baking dish. Put a ribbon of sour cream across the middle of the stalks. Sprinkle bread crumbs on this ribbon. Dribble 3 tbsp. melted butter over heads of asparagus. Reheat in a 350° oven for 10 minutes.

May

Once you have cooked a couple of pounds of asparagus, it is available in the refrigerator for incorporating into a variety of dishes, cold and hot. Served as a separate course (and really it should be), it can be dressed with a plain vinaigrette sauce or a somewhat different sauce made of 8 oz. of whipped cream cheese mixed with a hard-boiled egg yolk, 2 tbsp. Dijon mustard, a little oil, lemon juice and chopped chives.

The stalks are handsome on pieces of anchovy-buttered toast sprinkled with lemon butter and a bit of sieved egg yolk. To get two meals for the price of one with this vegetable, you can use the stalks for a pudding and purée the bright green tips with a plain Béchamel sauce to pour over another vegetable, such as cauliflower. Or you can wrap whole asparagus stalks in ham slices and cover them with a cheese-flavored cream sauce.

Asparagus Pudding

1 cup coarse bread or cracker crumbs
1 tsp. grated onion
1 tbsp. minced parsley
1 tsp. salt
   freshly ground pepper
4 tbsp. butter
4 cups cooked asparagus
   cut in 1-inch lengths
2 eggs
2 cups milk or half and half
   chopped chives

Melt butter and sauté crumbs, onion, parsley, salt and pepper for 5 minutes. Beat eggs and milk together. Add asparagus and crumb mixture. Pour into buttered bread tin. Bake at 375° for 30 minutes until pudding is set. Do not try to turn out of tin. Sprinkle each serving with chopped chives.

If you are stuck with a lot of skinny spears, and most people prefer the fat ones for cooking, just serve them raw, either with a curried mayonnaise for an hors d'oeuvre or cut up into nibblets in a salad.

RHUBARB

The leaves are extremely ornamental but toxic; the stem is highly edible and can be baked, stewed, made into cobblers, jelly, wine or marmalade. Pie-plant or rhubarb is a most refreshing spring tonic, although I didn't think so as a child when I was forced to drink a bitter combination of rhubarb and soda. Why wasn't it put into a deep-dish pie or just baked in a slow oven with ginger or orange peel? Sometimes there are valid reasons for a child's dislikes.

When you pick rhubarb, twist the stalk so as not to injure the crown, and put the leaves on the compost right away. Then hurry to cut up into 1½ to 2-inch lengths and bake it in a covered dish with one-fourth as much sweetening—either sugar or honey —and some interesting seasoning such as grated citrus peel or a spice. Bake it at 300° for about an hour and serve it for dessert with an applesauce cookie or for breakfast combined with bananas. Rhubarb can be stewed in a double boiler in the same way, with sugar and spices, only it won't have to cook as long. When done it will be soft and syrupy and a lovely shade of pink.

There is a recipe for a Rhubarb Tonic which by any other name would be more appealing. It is made very simply from 2 pounds of rhubarb cut into small pieces in 3 cups of water and stewed up for about 30 minutes or until it is very soft. Then strain this mixture, add about 6 tbsp. sugar, stirring to dissolve it, and chill. It reaches dizzying heights of gastronomy as an after-school drink when a large scoop of vanilla ice cream is added.

Vanilla ice cream also is good for a Rhubarb Cobbler or a Rhubarb and Strawberry Pie, although there are those who insist upon a good slice of Cheddar cheese with their fruit pies. Take your choice, but don't let spring go by without one or the other.

Put rhubarb in buttered baking dish. Dot butter over top and sprinkle in tapioca. Sprinkle cinnamon and lemon rind over top. In bowl, put flour, baking powder, salt and sugar. With fork or fingers mix in butter. Stir in gradually the milk to make a dough that holds together but is soft. Drop by spoonfuls onto rhubarb. Sprinkle with additional sugar. Bake at 400° for 30 minutes.

Rhubarb Cobbler

4 cups cooked, sweetened rhubarb
1 tbsp. butter
1 tbsp. quick tapioca
1 tbsp. grated lemon rind
1 tsp. ground cinnamon
2 cups flour
2 tsp. double-acting baking powder
½ tsp. salt
1 tbsp. sugar
4 tbsp. butter
   scant ¾ cup half & half or milk

Rhubarb and Strawberry Pie

2 cups rhubarb in 7-inch pieces
2 cups sliced strawberries
1½ cups sugar
   pinch of salt
⅓ cup flour
½ tsp. almond extract
2 tbsp. butter
1 recipe basic pie pastry

Mix together gently the strawberries, flour, rhubarb, sugar, salt and almond extract. Put into pastry-lined 9-inch pie pan. Dot with butter. Cover with pastry crust. Brush top crust with milk and sprinkle with sugar. Bake at 400° for 40-50 minutes until fruit is tender and crust is lightly browned.

It is interesting to experiment with fruits just to find out if they do other things as well as being desserts. One year when we were especially flooded with rhubarb, I tried a sauce for chicken and was pleasantly surprised with the results!

Chicken with Rhubarb Sauce

  1 fryer, cut up
1½ cups rhubarb in 7-inch pieces
  2 tbsp. sugar
  4 tbsp. honey
  1 tsp. salt
  1 cup orange juice
  ¼ cup lemon juice
  1 tbsp. arrowroot or potato flour dissolved in 3 tbsp. cold water

Cook rhubarb in orange juice until very soft. Strain through sieve. Add other ingredients and cook until sugar and honey are dissolved. Reserve ¼ cup of mixture. To remaining sauce add arrowroot flour dissolved in cold water. Stir until thick and glossy.
Brown chicken pieces in butter. Remove to casserole. Pour over thickened sauce. Bake uncovered at 350° for 40 minutes. Stir reserved rhubarb sauce into casserole and serve.

It is possible to force the spring growth of your rhubarb plants by putting barrels or open-ended boxes around them so they will reach for the light and grow taller, faster. You might note this in your calendar of things to do early in the spring because by the time someone notices the rhubarb it will be too late for forcing.

May

MINT

Your mint bed should be unfurling its tightly curled leaves this month. The new growth seems stronger in flavor and smell than it does later in the season, but perhaps our taste buds are fresher and more alive from the long winter. Dried mint is a very poor substitute for the real thing, yet we tend not to use the fresh for much except drinks or a garnish.

Not that I am deprecating iced tea, which we drink by the gallon all summer long. This recipe comes from a Southern friend who says that it probably is related somewhere along the line to Mint Juleps. It seems that half her family drank mint juleps while the other half drank iced tea. The basic principle is to bruise the mint leaves with the sugar, using a mortar and pestle or bowl and wooden spoon. Then add sugar and lemon juice.

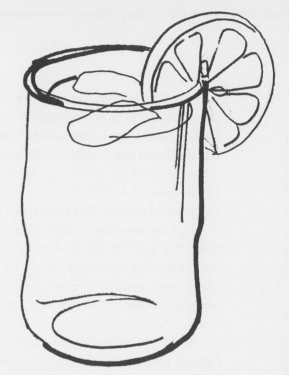

Iced Tea

  2 qts. strong hot tea
  1 large bunch fresh mint
  ½ cup lemon juice
1½ cups sugar
  ¼ cup orange juice (optional)

Bruise mint with sugar slightly. Stir in lemon juice and orange juice if desired. Add this mixture to tea while it is hot. Leave for 1 hour and strain.

There are so many varieties of mint that, if you can keep them all under control, it is fun to have a variegated mint bed. The roots have wanderlust, however, and you will find mint poking its head up in the most unlikely spots if you don't contain it with edging put deep down in the soil.

Mint is associated with Mid-Eastern cuisine, and one of the looked-forward-to summer dishes is a salad made of wheat pilaf or groats and mint. It must be very healthful, and I know that it is delicious, with a chewy, nutty texture and flavor. Speaking of health foods, I have never been over-fond of yogurt, but as a salad dressing combined with mint and cucumbers it makes a most palatable side dish for a curry and a somewhat unusual salad to take on a picnic with a cold lamb loaf. Mint has a springlike freshness that goes well in eggplant dishes. And try a small touch in fresh peas or carrots. A large touch would be too much noticed, however.

A fresh pea soup flavored with mint and tarragon is a good beginning for a summer meal, especially when served in white china soup plates on bright yellow mats.

Tabbouli

  1   cup wheat pilaf or groats
  1   tsp. salt
1¼   cups water
  ½   cup finely chopped mint
  4   cups finely chopped parsley
  1   cup finely chopped spring onion
  ¾   cup chopped peeled tomato
  ½   cup olive oil
  ¼   cup fresh lemon juice
  ½   tsp. salt
  ½   tsp. pepper

Bring salted water to a boil. Add pilaf, cover, and remove from heat. After ½ hour water will be absorbed. Fluff with fork. Stir in the remaining ingredients. Season to taste. Let stand at room temperature for a few hours. Serve on lettuce leaves or watercress.

May

Mint Yoghurt Salad Dressing

- 1 cucumber
- 1 green pepper
- ¼ small white onion
  salt
- 1 tsp. sugar
- 1 tbsp. lemon juice
- 1 cup plain yoghurt
- 1 tbsp. oil
- ½ tsp. salt
- ½ tsp. sugar
- ¼ tsp. wine vinegar
- 2 tsp. chopped mint

Peel and seed cucumber, Cut into matchstick strips. Sprinkle with salt and sugar. Cut a green pepper into matchstick strips. Sprinkle with a few very thin onion rings. Season with salt and lemon juice. Mix cucumber and pepper together. In yoghurt stir oil, salt, sugar, vinegar and mint. Mix dressing with vegetables just before serving.

May

CHIVES

The chive plant already may have produced its pretty purple flowers and is on its second growth. In any case, you must have lots of chives. A good way to use some of them is in a pretty but quick-and-easy recipe for chicken breasts that might be included in your Memorial Day repertoire. Serve it with brown rice for a change, asparagus vinaigrette, and a rich sugary rhubarb crisp. Come rain or shine, you'll be all set.

Chicken Sauté

1 fryer, cut up
  flour, salt, paprika
4 tbsp. butter
2 tbsp. chopped mixed fresh herbs
  (parsley, chives, tarragon, thyme)
¼ cup chicken broth
¼ cup dry white wine
⅔ cup sour cream
1 tbsp. flour
2 tbsp. chopped chives

Dredge chicken in flour mixed with salt and paprika. Do this by putting seasonings in paper bag and shaking chicken parts in it. Brown chicken quickly in butter and 1 tbsp. oil. Sprinkle mixed herbs over chicken, add broth and cover. Cook for 20 minutes over medium heat until done. Remove chicken to warm platter. Add wine, blending with juices in pan. Add sour cream mixed with flour and chives. Stir until heated through. Pour over chicken and serve.

May

Memorial Day should find your garden in prime condition with everything in and lots of green showing. The rows are neat and tidy with paths of mulch between. The lettuce and carrots both need thinning; if the beets were carefully planted they do not. The shallots should have numerous green sprouts coming out of their tops; the garlic fronds are tall and strong; the English cress threatening to engulf the rest of your herbs should be cut back sharply or removed altogether.

All in all, it is a nice feeling to know that from here on it is all easy going, barring what the insurance men refer to as an "act of God."

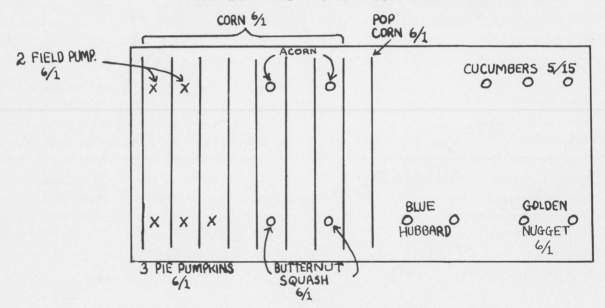

THE BLANCHARD'S VINE AND CORN PATCH 24' x 8'

June

"WE JUST don't seem to have a real spring anymore" really means that we go right from chilly nights and cool days into nights warm enough to leave windows open and to days that are hot. The change seems to be harder on us than on the plants, which have been waiting through the spring rains for the warm sunshine needed to help their blossoms along. Now take a good look at the peas to see if there are white blossoms showing.

This is the first month when the gardener is eyed with envy. While others are still haunting the markets, we are eating our own crisp lettuce and radishes with the enjoyment that comes from having worked for them. Perhaps one of the best ways to convince a person of gardening's value is to take him into an early June garden and let him pick the young radish and the silky Buttercrunch lettuce and eat them on the spot. Then, if you have to say "Here is your reason for gardening," he is a lost cause. If, on the other hand, he devours a whole head of Buttercrunch and then starts in on the Romaine, you know that you have a convert. He might even be willing to lend a hand with the work in return for more sustenance as the summer wears on.

Pick your produce young and small. The commercial growers don't pick their beans three inches and their carrots four inches long. They can't afford to, but you can and should. Plant another fifteen-foot row of beans about the third week in June. You should also replant your carrots, radishes and beets. An easy system for keeping track of lettuce is to replace as you pick. Start picking from the end of a row and when three feet are empty, put in more seeds.

Tie up your tomato plants this month, using pieces of cloth or old nylons rather than string, so as not to cut into the stalks. Don't forget, there should be one main stem to a tomato plant, so nip off all of the other stems or "suckers." In this way you force the growth into one place, getting a better and earlier yield of fruit.

66

June

PEAS

Peas used to be a seasonal vegetable. The traditional meal for the Fourth of July was salmon and peas and strawberries. As far as I'm concerned, peas are still seasonal. There are frozen peas and there also are canned peas. But there is no vegetable quite like fresh peas. There is no moment in the gardening year, perhaps because we are not yet surfeited with freshness, that equals the moment when you pull the first full pod carefully off the vine, crack the end with your thumb, split it down the side and roll those perfect sweet small peas into your mouth. Why cook them, you think? And you are almost right. But if you have planted enough, there will be about two weeks of eating peas. So it is nice to have a bit of variety in preparation after the first excitement wears off.

Pea-picking time demands cooperation from all members of the family and any guests who happen to be around. Peas cannot be left on the vines too long, for there is an optimum period of excellence during which they must be picked, podded, and cooked or frozen.

After many years, I still haven't decided whether I want the first meal of peas to be lunch or dinner. But that first meal always is cereal bowls of peas with butter and salt. What goes with them is not too important, although bread, cheese and fruit are pleasant accompaniments.

For plain cooked peas I use the French method, which is virtually waterless and which points up their finest flavor: Line the bottom of a heavy pot with wet lettuce leaves. Put in a few pea pods. Then pour in the peas. Dot with butter and sprinkle a little sugar on them. Never salt peas until they are cooked, though sugar brings out their flavor. Top with a few more lettuce leaves. Cover tightly. Put the pan over high heat and when you hear a bubbling, within one or two minutes, turn to medium heat. Let peas cook for five minutes, then test for doneness. Add more butter if necessary. Take out the lettuce and the pea pods and serve with salt and pepper. It may come close to being the best thing you have eaten since pea-picking time last year.

As this is primarily an in-season book, I am not going into freezing or preserving much, but the one vegetable that we purposely plant too much of at one time is peas. We do this because we really do not like hot weather peas enough to give up the garden space to them. Then why don't we plant just enough peas to eat in season? Because we do have space to spare early in the season, and because we want to hedge against the possible loss of such a fine crop; and also we freeze some. There is safety in numbers here.

Children love to shell peas, especially if you make it a family project and don't regale them with too many stories about the old days on the farm. Start them off slowly, building gradually up to the night when the podding and freezing goes on into the wee hours. I find that if I freeze a few pounds a day all through the short season, it is not too much of a job, except at the very end when we pull

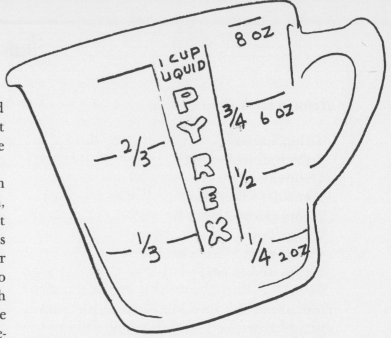

the vines and discover all those we missed. You can blanch the peas if you wish, but we just pod and bag them, and in this way they don't stick together in the packages.

Peas are eaten in Italy a lot, a country where they love to serve vegetables in their pristine glory unadulterated by sauces. One distinctly Italian recipe that we are fond of is a risotto using peas tossed in at the last moment. Another makes much of the distinctly Mediterranean flavorings of garlic and oil, with bits of chopped ham added.

Risotto with Peas

4 tbsp. butter
2 tbsp. minced onion
1 cup raw rice
½ cup dry white wine
2 cups chicken broth
2 tbsp. butter
4 tbsp. grated Parmesan cheese
2 cups cooked peas

Heat butter in saucepan. Cook onion until soft. Add rice and stir until translucent, 5 minutes. Add wine and stir in hot broth. Cover and cook until broth is absorbed and rice is done but not mushy. Stir in additional butter, peas, and Parmesan cheese.

Italian Peas and Prosciutto

2 lbs. of peas in pods
1 clove garlic, minced
3 tbsp. butter
1 tbsp. oil
½ cup chopped Italian prosciutto ham or regular smoked ham
2 tbsp. bouillon
2 tbsp. chopped parsley

Heat butter and oil together. Sauté garlic briefly. Stir in ham. Pod and cook the peas in as little water as possible until just tender. Add the peas to the ham and garlic. Add bouillon. Cover and simmer together until done. Sprinkle with parsley.

Puréed peas are too much like baby food when served as a separate vegetable, but you can make other good uses for peas that were overlooked on the first pickings. A fresh green pea soup, served either hot or cold, is a wonderful beginning to a meal, or it may take the place of your vegetable course.

June

Fresh Green Pea Soup

1½ cups peas and 5 pods
 ½ tsp. fresh tarragon, chopped
 1 tsp. fresh mint, chopped
 3 cups chicken broth
 2 tbsp. butter
 1 tbsp. flour
 ½ cup chopped celery
 2 tbsp. chopped onion
 ½ cup medium cream

Simmer peas, pods, onion and celery in chicken broth for 15 minutes. Place in blender with butter, flour and herbs. Blend until smooth. Strain into saucepan. Bring to boil and simmer 10 minutes. Chill. Before serving stir in cream and season to taste with salt.

There are so many things to do with peas. It doesn't seem that the season is long enough to try them all, especially allowing for the many meals when just plain fresh peas in butter or in a little cream may be all you want.

This sounds as though I am advocating a meatless meal and in truth I am. If for reasons of economy or health or just plain boredom with preparing meat, if you wish to try a vegetarian diet occasionally, now is the season. It is the time to make the most of your vegetables; to make them the most important part of a meal, to gloat over them, to glorify them, to become addicted to the freshest flavors you can possibly have.

There is a purity to fresh fruits and vegetables that can be appreciated only when they are savored for themselves alone. And there is nothing more attractive at table than a platter of vegetables in different shapes and colors. With breads and cheeses and fruits of the season, you can provide an interesting, unusual and also a well-balanced meal, satisfying to anyone.

June

STRAWBERRIES

There are many who would agree with Sydney Smith's statement that "doubtless God could have made a better berry than the strawberry but He never did." A perfect strawberry indeed is a most beautiful sight, and when it is picked from the patch, sun-ripened and warm, full of sweet juices, it is a tribute to the good things that come in the month of June. It's also a tribute to the work you have done, because a strawberry bed is not the easiest thing to maintain.

The strawberry, according to an old cookbook, has amazing curative powers for gout, if that happens to be troubling you, and if the acid in strawberries does not agree with you, this same book suggests adding a little cayenne pepper to aid digestion.

Rightfully the strawberry should stand alone, just served in all its pristine glory with a bowl of powdered sugar for dipping. A very pretty dessert is effected by setting the berries, preferably all of the same size, on a bed of powdered sugar in a round white low-sided dish with their green caps up. No spoon is needed; the guests help themselves with their fingers.

A simple and attractive dessert is made up from a meringue shell filled with berries and whipped cream. You do have to put it together just before serving, but all the separate parts can be prepared ahead of time.

Try not to wash your strawberries; if they are slightly dirty, brush them off. Water will make them soggy and then they cannot be served whole. I had a friend who used to rinse her strawberries in Port wine. Then she marinated them in 1 cup of sour cream, 1 teaspoon of vanilla, and a quarter cup of the wine they had been rinsed in. After chilling for a few hours, she served the dessert garnished with ice cubes that had berries frozen into them—nice for a cool June night when the dessert wasn't apt to melt quickly. Since this friend had a very large strawberry bed, much of her time was spent devising new ways of using the berries, in addition to jam, jelly, tutti frutti and the more usual ways. One interesting combination that she came up with used Kirsch, pistachio nuts and her own version of Crème Fraiche.

Fraises en Vasque

Sprinkle strawberries lightly with powdered sugar and cherry brandy. Chill for several hours. Pour on Crème Fraiche and sprinkle with chopped pistachio nuts. Crème Fraiche: Beat 1 cup heavy cream until it thickens a little, but do not whip. Blend in ½ cup sour cream. Let stand a few hours.

Now is the time to start your Rum Pot. Putting this recipe together through the summer months, adding the fruits as they ripen, makes one very aware of how much the orchard has to offer. It also solves a few Christmas present problems when you bottle it. Suggest to friends that it will make a good Christmas Eve dessert sauce served warm over ice cream. And for New Year's Eve, heat the Tutti Frutti in a chafing dish at the table and flame it with a jigger of rum or cognac. When flaming any liquor, warm it first so that it will ignite faster.

Tutti Frutti

Put a pint of brandy or rum into a large stone crock. As each fruit comes into season, starting with strawberries, add it to the crock. For each 2 cups of fruit, put in 2 cups of sugar. Cover tightly and put in a cool place. Stir daily until all fruit has been added. Stone cherries, seed grapes and pit peaches, plums and apricots. Do not use apples, bananas, or citrus fruits. Store for 3 months before using, then seal in jars if you wish.

Whatever happened to the old-fashioned strawberry festival? In our small New England town it was the social event of the season, and everyone came to eat his share of the June berry crop in the form of strawberry shortcake—the real thing with mashed, sweetened berries dripping juice heaped on a plain buttered biscuit, with a cap of real whipped cream crowning the top. No artificially-flavored spongecake here. I still serve shortcake once during the season and make it with biscuits.

Our grandmothers knew their shortcakes: an unsweetened biscuit enhances the natural flavor of the berry while a cake kills it. It is good, also, to serve your berries in plain or lightly sweetened whipped cream or fold them into a syllabub faintly flavored with wine.

Strawberry Syllabub

½ **cup powdered sugar**
1 **cup heavy cream**
2 **egg whites**
2 **tbsp. medium dry sherry**
1 **quart strawberries**

Add half of the sugar to cream; whip until stiff. Beat egg whites stiff with remaining sugar. Combine cream and whites and blend together. Add wine. Pour over fruit in bowl.

As with peas, it is hard to know where to stop with recipes for strawberries. Fruit juice brings out their flavor nicely, so you might simply cover a quart of them with powdered sugar and pour a half cup of orange juice over them just before serving. Imperfect berries can be crushed with sugar and used for sauce or folded with a little orange liqueur into softened vanilla ice cream and packed into a ring mold. When you unmold it, garnish with whole strawberries and lemon balm leaves.

One of the prettiest and most elegant desserts in the world is a fruit tart, really a party pie—one with a fluted edge and no pastry cover. The basic recipe can be used for any fruit in season, changing your flavor of jelly glaze to fit the fruit.

June

Strawberry Tart

Pastry: 1½ cups flour
1½ sticks butter
4 tbsp. powdered sugar

Mix all together and press into a 9-inch fluted-edge tart pan. Bake at 425° for 12-15 minutes. Cool.

Pastry Cream: ¼ cup sugar
⅓ cup flour
3 egg yolks
1 cup milk
1 tsp. vanilla

Mix sugar, flour, egg yolks and a little milk in saucepan. Beat in rest of milk and cook, stirring, over medium heat until mixture comes to a boil. Remove from heat. Cool and add vanilla. Chill. Hull 1 quart of strawberries.

To assemble, fill pastry shell with pastry cream. Arrange berries stem side down on top, completely covering the pastry cream. Then brush with glaze. Melt ½ cup currant jelly with 2 tbsp. Kirsch, cognac, or orange juice. When liquid, brush over top of tart, making sure to fill in all spaces between berries. Refrigerate until ½ hour before serving.

LETTUCES

Romaine is firm and large-leafed, the heads standing like proud soldiers in a row. Buttercrunch is fat and buttery, and the leaf lettuces are light and airy. It's salad every day, and now you can see why I advised earlier to make short plantings frequently. A little bit of lettuce goes a long way when you are sprinkling the seeds around.

The best salads are made from a combination of greens, for color as well as texture and flavor contrasts. The dressing is important, as is the method of preparation. We have all eaten wilted lettuces that just got drowned in the dressing. You must start with completely dry greens. Having washed everything thoroughly, dry it all in towels and put it in the refrigerator still wrapped in the towel.

My Vinaigrette Dressing recipe is simple and its success depends on just one thing: good ingredients. I use my own herb vinegar and a good brand of Italian olive oil. If you prefer, mix in a little French oil. It is lighter but quite a bit more expensive. The proportions are: 1 tsp. salt, 1 tsp. sugar, 1 tsp. pepper, 1 tsp. Dijon mustard, ¼ cup vinegar, and ¾ cup oil. You may vary these proportions if you prefer a sharper dressing, and you should certainly add a tbsp. of fresh herbs in the summer. A good basic mixture of herbs is in the proportions of: 3 to 4 tbsp. chopped parsley, 1 tbsp. chopped chives, 1 tbsp. chopped tarragon, 1 tbsp. chopped lemon balm, 2 tsp. chopped watercress. This *fines herbes* mixture can be added to a plain melted butter sauce for fish, a cream sauce for chicken, or it may be incorporated very successfully into a plain omelet.

Thank goodness for fresh parsley. I toss a handful of it into every salad, which is made up in the bowl ahead of time, minus dressing, a damp paper towel placed over the top. It stays in the refrigerator until dinner time because a hot kitchen will wilt the enthusiasm of any lettuce leaf.

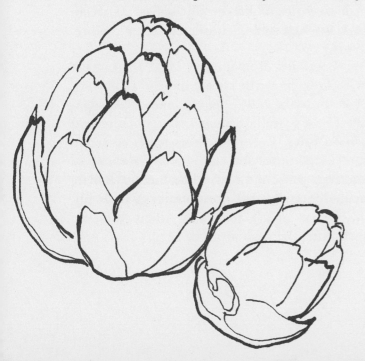

As we move into warmer weather, consider more hearty salads. Serve them with a hot broth, bacon-spiked corn bread, and a fresh banana cake for a summer dinner any family will praise. Caesar Salad is one of the best because it makes full use of those beautiful strong heads of Romaine, which will thrive until fall if you keep replanting. Romaine also is considered to have more flavor and vitamins than any other salad green.

So on to a robust Caesar Salad which supposedly was created by a chef in Tijuana, Mexico, although we tend to credit it to California cuisine, where it usually is served as a first course.

Caesar Salad

2 bunches Romaine lettuce
2 large garlic cloves
3 anchovies
1¼ tsp. dry mustard
½ tsp. salt
   freshly ground pepper
   dash of Worcestershire
1 tbsp. tarragon vinegar
2 tbsp. oil
   juice of ½ lemon
3 tbsp. grated Parmesan cheese
1 raw egg yolk

Wash and dry Romaine. In salad bowl, mash with fork the garlic cloves and the anchovies. Add mustard, salt, pepper and Worcestershire. Mix well. Stir in vinegar, oil, and lemon juice. Let stand until ready to serve. Break up lettuce and add to bowl. Add cheese and egg yolk and toss so that every leaf is coated. You may add croutons if you wish.

June

SPINACH

Now is the moment of truth as far as spinach is concerned. Probably you have been tossing it into salads for the last couple of weeks. But now comes the true test: spinach for itself alone.

Proper cooking is the secret. Now we know that spinach should be just barely cooked. It used to be boiled to death in quarts of water and then served limp like seaweed, with vinegar on it. If you are doing large quantities of spinach or other greens, you can dry them in the spin-dry cycle of your washing machine. Just put the wet leaves in an old pillowcase (one that you don't want to use again) with a few paper towels. Tie the top of the case securely and put it in your machine, setting the dial for cold rinse and spin-dry cycle. Spinach does especially well under this treatment and it is a very satisfactory feeling to look at a large amount of such beautiful material in the crisper all set to go.

I put the still-wet spinach leaves into a large pot. Cover the pot and turn the heat to high. In approximately three minutes the spinach has wilted down and is ready to be drained and dressed with butter, salt, pepper and nutmeg, or to be chopped and creamed or chopped and made into a soufflé or incorporated into an unusual tart. Even spinach-haters like it when it is partially disguised. Besides, if you planted it, you will love it.

June

Spinach Soufflé

3 tbsp. butter
3 tbsp. flour
½ cup chicken broth
½ cup milk
1 cup well-drained chopped spinach
2 shallots, minced
5 egg yolks
6 egg whites
½ cup grated Parmesan cheese
1 tsp. salt
½ tsp. pepper
¼ tsp. nutmeg

Sauté shallots in butter in saucepan about 1 minute. Stir in flour and cook until golden and bubbly. Add liquids all at once and stir until smooth and thick. Season. Add egg yolks, blending well. Stir in spinach and ¼ cup cheese. Beat whites until stiff. Fold into spinach mixture. Pour into 1½-quart soufflé dish and sprinkle remaining cheese on top. Bake at 325° until firm, about 30 minutes.

Spinach Tart

2 lbs. spinach
¼ lb. Feta cheese (Greek)
½ lb. Ricotta or large-curd cottage cheese
3 eggs
½ cup minced onion
2 shallots
½ cup cream
4 tbsp. butter
nutmeg
salt
pepper

Cook spinach. Drain in colander and press with hand until most of moisture is out. Squeeze if necessary, since you do not want any moisture leaking from the spinach into the casserole. Sauté minced shallots and onion in butter. Add to spinach. Beat together eggs and ricotta or cottage cheese. Add feta cheese, crumbled, to the spinach. Combine two mixtures and add cream to moisten. Season well with salt, pepper and nutmeg. Pour into shallow greased baking dish. Bake for 30 minutes at 375°.

June

As for your leftover spinach—and there is usually one in the family who cannot be persuaded of its goodness—use it for making Florentine dishes, the name applied to anything served on a bed of spinach. This can be poached eggs, fillets of fish, or a poached chicken breast. Just pour a little cheese sauce over any one of these and you have brunch, lunch, or dinner all set.

Spinach salad with raw mushrooms is a very pleasant change, or you might try a wilted spinach salad; and that's just what it is.

Wilted Spinach

1 lb. fresh spinach leaves, washed and dried
6 pieces bacon
1 hard-boiled egg yolk
¼ cup vinegar
1 tbsp. brown sugar
  salt and pepper
1 tbsp. chopped scallions

Cook bacon slices until crisp. Drain and crumble. Pour off all but 3 tbsp. bacon fat. Mix sugar and spices with vinegar. Into warm bacon fat stir vinegar. Bring to a boil and pour over bowl of spinach leaves. Sprinkle sieved egg yolk, scallions, and crumbled bacon on top. Toss and serve immediately.

Once started on spinach, it is hard to stop —it has such wonderful possibilities for creative cooking. Have you ever made a spinach soufflé roll and served it cold with a curried minced chicken filling or hot with a creamed mushroom filling? Here I have varied the basic recipe by adding puréed artichoke hearts to make a somewhat lighter roll without a dense spinach flavor.

Spinach Artichoke Roll

1½ lbs. spinach, cooked, drained dry, and finely chopped
1 15-oz. can artichoke hearts packed in brine
5 eggs, separated
6 tbsp. butter, melted
1 tsp. salt
½ tsp. pepper
¼ tsp. nutmeg

Place spinach in bowl. Put artichoke hearts in blender with 3 tbsp. melted butter. Blend into purée. You may have to stop the blender and push mixture down with a rubber spatula. It will not be a completely smooth purée. Mix artichokes with spinach. Stir in remaining butter, egg yolks and seasonings. Beat whites stiff with extra ½ tsp. salt. Fold whites into spinach mixture. Prepare a 10 by 15-inch jelly roll pan: grease pan, cover with a piece of waxed paper long enough to cover both ends of pan, and grease paper well.

Spread soufflé mixture in pan. Bake at 375° for 18 minutes. Turn roll out on clean towel. Let rest 5 minutes. Strip off waxed paper. Roll up while warm. Unroll and cool.

Spread the roll with herb cheese and roll it up for hors d'oeuvres; or spread with finely chopped creamed mushrooms and serve with Hollandaise sauce for a hot vegetable accompaniment to lamb or beef. Try it spread with finely chopped chicken mixed with a curry mayonnaise for a picnic.

The roll may be cut in half if you have trouble fitting it on a platter. It may be frozen flat and unfilled.

June

CARROTS

I'll try not to become tiresome about the subject of appearance of food, but it is so important. One way to secure interesting visual results with a vegetable is to change your method of preparing it. For instance, grate raw carrots and bake them in heavy cream, butter, and a whiff of ground ginger; or cook them until they are very soft and rice them, stirring in a pat of butter, salt and pepper, and a grating of raw onion. Perhaps you have one of those fancy cutting gadgets that makes waffled vegetables. Use it when preparing carrots for a stew, instead of cutting them into chunks. Then serve them separately, as a bright spot of color, instead of hiding them in the brown gravy.

As a matter fact, I usually don't include the vegetables in the stew; it doesn't seem fair to the vegetables. I put the meat in its rich gravy in the center of a large platter and surround it with the appropriate vegetables —peas, carrots, beans, onions, and potatoes— each cooked separately. It's a lovely edible still-life and much more appealing than a dark brown pot mixture.

The natural sweetness in carrots is a reason, however, for including them in the soup or stew pot, since they act as natural tenderizers. There is a lovely dish named Orange

Carrots which can be made in June with tiny whole carrots from the garden. Or, if some have escaped your notice and are on their way to becoming quite large, just slice them very thinly on the bias, parboil for five minutes in salted water, then cook the thin slices in butter with a sprinkling of sugar or honey in a covered heavy saucepan over very low heat until the carrots are tender and glazed.

Orange Carrots

4½ **cups small carrots or carrot sticks, cooked**
3 **tbsp. orange juice**
1½ **tbsp. sugar**
4 **tbsp. butter**
6 **cloves**
1 **tsp. salt**
    chopped parsley

Combine in saucepan the orange juice, sugar, butter and whole cloves. Cook until butter is melted and sauce thickens slightly. Remove cloves and add salt. Add carrots and warm through. Sprinkle with parsley before serving.

Just to prove that carrots can be a pleasant entrance part of a meal, you might try a carrot soup made by blending leftover carrots with a bit of cooked rice (for body), some chicken broth, minced onion, and cream in the blender. Heat this and grate a little raw carrot over the top.

My final suggestion for carrots would be a salad, a nice crispy touch to a seasonal meal. Grate some carrots on the medium to large holes of your grater and mix into this some mayonnaise, sour cream, Dijon mustard and lemon juice. Taste as you go and take it easy on the mustard until you decide just how sharp you want it. Add salt and pepper to please yourself, and when you serve the salad be sure to put a topknot of parsley on each helping.

June

BEETS

Before we leave the merry month of June, the delightful month of radishes and roses and early summer savories, let us look to the beets which, right now, are a lovely size. They are not too big but just right to serve whole in salad or baked in their skins or grated and sautéed with butter or sauced in orange or made into that smooth glowing Russian concoction, Borscht. See how many things you can do with the lowly beet? And there are more.

The first thing to remember about cooking beets is that they should be used when they are young and tender. Get in the habit of adding sugar to the water in which they are cooked. This brings out the natural sweetness in the root. If you bake beets in their skins in a 325° oven for an hour, they will keep their flavor and color nicely. Serve them with butter or sour cream and chopped chives. Make your own pickled beets to use as part of a smorgasbord with various meats and fish. Or combine them with walnuts and slivered celery for a tasty side dish. Beets add a most important ingredient to a meal: color. But remember to drain off the juice if they are to be served on the same plate as other foods.

Pickled Beets

2 cups cooked, sliced beets
1 medium onion, sliced thinly
½ cup herb vinegar
1 tsp. salt
1 tsp. sugar
1 tsp. horseradish

Put hot beets into bowl. Cover with onion rings. Mix together the vinegar, horseradish, salt and sugar. Pour over beets and let marinate for a few hours. Chill.

Beet and Celery Salad

2 cups sliced, cooked beets
1 cup diced raw celery
2 tbsp. lemon juice
6 tbsp. olive oil
½ tsp. salt
½ tsp. pepper
1 tsp. sugar
1 hard-boiled egg yolk, sieved

Arrange cold sliced beets on a platter. Cover with celery. Mix together the lemon juice, oil and seasonings with a fork or whisk until well blended. Pour over salad. Garnish with sieved egg yolk.

Sautéed Beets

12 raw beets, peeled
6 tbsp. butter
1 tsp. salt
　 freshly ground pepper
½ cup sour cream
1 tbsp. lemon juice

Grate raw beets coarsely on grater. Put into frying pan with butter. Sauté over medium heat until tender. Add salt, pepper and lemon juice. Stir in sour cream and heat through.

Beets in Orange Sauce

12 beets, cooked and sliced
½ cup sugar
1 tsp. cornstarch
½ cup orange juice
1 tbsp. lemon juice
3 tbsp. orange marmalade
2 tbsp. butter

Combine sugar, cornstarch, orange juice, and lemon juice in small saucepan and boil until clear and thick. Stir in marmalade and butter and blend well. Add beets and heat all together.

Final note: if you find some really tiny beets, smaller than cherry tomatoes, boil, chill, and serve them on toothpicks for a cocktail party with a bowl of sour cream heavily spiked with horseradish.

June

PEPPERS

Thank heaven we don't have to pick a peck of peppers all at once. They come in twos and threes which is enough to cope with. The shiny bright green globes can stand on their own nicely enough as a vegetable or main course, although they also do very well when added to scrambled eggs, omelets, salads, or combined with other summer vegetables in some of the innumerable mélanges we treat ourselves to during this season. Unfortunately for many, "stuffed peppers" were overdone, in more ways than one, during childhood, so we are inclined to eye them with distrust. But, when not overcooked and when filled with a spicy mixture of herbed rice, anchovies, and garlic, and presented with a Greek lemon and egg sauce, the sweet pepper is at its beautiful best.

To peel peppers: roast them in a 450° oven for 10 minutes. Then they may be seeded, cut into strips, and marinated in a well-seasoned lemon juice and oil dressing. Sprinkle with a few capers.

Bright green pepper rings are a pretty addition to a salad, and to keep their color just blanch them in boiling water for one minute, then plunge them into cold water immediately. Peppers can be stuffed with other vegetables, such as corn or eggplant, or stewed with bacon, tomatoes and onion, or fried and served with sausage links or veal cutlets. Make use of them now while they are part of our garden produce and let next winter take care of itself.

Greek Stuffed Peppers

6 sweet green peppers
1 clove garlic, minced
2 tsp. chopped fresh basil
2 tbsp. chopped parsley
3 tbsp. oil
1 cup raw rice
2 tomatoes, peeled and chopped
1 cup chicken broth
3 eggs
  juice of 1 lemon

Parboil peppers for 10 minutes. Plunge into cold water. Dry. Take off tops and hollow out. Heat oil in frying pan and add garlic, basil, and parsley. Sauté briefly—5 minutes. Add rice, sauté until translucent—about 5 minutes. Add chopped tomatoes and ½ cup chicken broth. Simmer, stirring occasionally, until liquid is almost absorbed. Fill peppers with rice mixture. Place in baking dish. Pour rest of broth into dish, adding water so liquid is 1 inch over bottom of dish. Bake at 350° for 45 minutes. Remove from oven. In small bowl, beat three eggs with lemon juice. Pour off ¾ cup liquid from baking dish and very slowly add it to the eggs, beating constantly. When thoroughly blended, pour sauce over peppers and put back in oven for 5 minutes.

Sautéed Peppers

3 green peppers, cut in strips
4 slices bacon, diced
2 tomatoes, peeled and chopped
1 tsp. salt
  freshly ground pepper

Sauté bacon until done. Add peppers to pan and sauté until limp. Add tomatoes, salt and pepper. Cover and cook until done, about 10 minutes. You may add a dash of hot pepper sauce if you wish. Or scramble some eggs right in the pan.

June

HERBS

Certain basic long-lasting things come from my herb garden that are essential to the pantry shelf—three to be exact: pesto, herb vinegars, and basil jelly. The first, pesto, is a lovely green sauce that is the very essence of Italy in any dish it graces. It is redolent of garlic and sweet basil and goes on pasta, in vegetable soup, on mushrooms, in scrambled eggs, with most vegetables, and is mixed into salad dressing. I make it in large batches through the summer and freeze it in small plastic bags. If pine nuts are hard to find, substitute walnuts rather than not make it at all, but you must have fresh basil.

Pesto

    5 garlic cloves, crushed
 1¾ cup fresh basil leaves
  ⅓ cup grated Parmesan cheese
  ¼ cup pine nuts or walnuts
6 to 8 tbsp. olive oil

Put basil leaves, garlic cloves, cheese, and nuts in blender container. Add a small amount of oil and blend, turning motor on and off and pushing mixture down with rubber spatula. Add oil gradually until the mixture is a thick, smooth sauce.

Herb vinegars are made simply by putting a few sprigs of any herb in a bottle of vinegar, corking it and leaving it to mull for three weeks. At the end of the period you may remove the herbs or not, as you choose. One of my favorite combinations is 3 sprigs mint, 4 sprigs basil, and one garlic clove in a quart bottle of cider vinegar. You may substitute dill for the basil. Tarragon vinegar, the essential ingredient of a true Béarnaise sauce, is made by putting a large spray of tarragon in a bottle of white vinegar. If you wish to have wine vinegar, just pour out about one-quarter of the vinegar and replace it with a dry white wine. Other interesting vinegars are made by combining basil and oregano and a few whole peppercorns in a bottle of red wine vinegar, lemon thyme and rosemary in white wine vinegar or chives and lemon balm in white vinegar. Don't forget that the herbs themselves are usable; they have just been preserved in the vinegar.

The last item on my list of pretty edibles that I would like to have over the winter is basil jelly. Pale green in color and more delicate in flavor than mint jelly, it is a pleasant accompaniment to lamb or poultry.

Basil Jelly

- 2 cups water
- ¾ cup cider vinegar
- ¼ cup lemon juice
- 1 cup basil leaves (packed)
- 6 cups sugar
- 6 tbsp. liquid pectin
  green food coloring
- 10 lemon balm or verbena leaves

Bring water, vinegar and lemon juice to boil in large pot. Bruise the basil leaves, add to pot, remove from heat, steep 20 minutes. Strain. Add sugar, return to heat and bring to full boil, stirring constantly until sugar is dissolved. When syrup is at full rolling boil, add pectin and boil for ½ minute. Remove from heat. Add a few drops of food coloring until syrup is a pale green. Place 2 lemon leaves in bottom of each sterilized jelly glass and pour in jelly. Cool and cover with layer of paraffin.

Note: to sterilize glasses, run through your dishwasher and leave in until ready to use.

Herbs sometimes do not do well indoors and professional growers will caution you against trying to grow them on your kitchen windowsill unless you have optimum conditions and a kelly green thumb. It is best to buy your plants each spring of the year and try to winter over things like rosemary and tarragon. Thyme and chives should come back, and oregano may. Lemon balm always returns in great abundance and its leaves can be used to decorate a cake plate or in a small bouquet of fragrance for the kitchen counter. When you are searching for garnishes, don't overlook the possibilities furnished by your herb garden, where there are beauty and color with which to decorate a platter.

If you wish to carry your rosemary through the winter, dig it up in the fall and put it in a good-sized pot. Try to keep it in a cool place and don't forget that it needs a lot of moisture. Put it in the shower at least once a week. If you have a humidifier, so much the better, but keep the plant away from heating units. Treat yourself to a leg of spring lamb and cook it long and slowly to produce a moist, slightly pink, but thoroughly cooked and beautifully flavored roast that is just as good the second night because it has not dried out.

Channel Island Lamb

Marinate a leg of lamb for 12-24 hours in 2 cups dry white wine and ½ cup oil. Turn occasionally. Remove lamb from marinade, dry, and trim off as much fat as possible. Chop together very fine 6 rosemary leaves, 1 large clove garlic, and 2 tsp. lemon rind. Make ½-inch deep slits in lamb leg with point of knife and stuff with mixture. Put on rack in roasting pan and place in preheated 300° oven. Set timer for 1 hour. At end of hour, turn heat down to 150°. Leave lamb in for at least 6 hours, more if you wish. Because the internal temperature of the lamb will not go above 150°, the meat will not overcook if it should stay in for another hour. If you wish to have roast lamb warm the next night, just put it in the oven at 150° for an hour.

Sage is a questionable item in many gardens. Most people find it too strong in flavor for their tastes and are always reminded (not pleasantly, it seems) of turkey stuffings and highly seasoned pork sausages. Strong it is, not only in flavor but in its grasp on life, as year after year it comes back after the bitterest of winters. Some years we use it out of the garden in January in a wonderful Italian recipe for chicken livers that was given to me by cookbook author Nika Hazelton.

Venetian Chicken Livers

1 lb. chicken livers
  salt and pepper
12 chopped fresh sage leaves
  or 1 tbsp. dried sage

¼ cup butter
2 slices bacon, diced
¼ cup dry white wine

Cut chicken livers into halves if they are large. Season with salt and pepper and coat with sage. Heat butter and bacon together in skillet. Sauté livers 5-6 minutes. Add white wine and simmer 2 minutes longer. Serve on spaghetti, rice, or polenta.

The herb cheese I mentioned a while back is one of those seasonal recipes that is worth waiting for, so do not try to make it in the winter with dried dill and frozen chives. It will be a great disappointment and just confirm the gardener's philosophy that there is a reason why we should stick to the seasons and enjoy each thing as it comes. Of course, it is pleasant to have a choice of vegetables all year round and not be limited, as our ancestors were, to the dull root staples, but how exciting to sample anew the "firsts" of each growing season as they come around, without benefit of can or freezer bag.

Herb Cheese

1 8-oz. package whipped cream cheese
1 clove of garlic
1½ tbsp. olive oil
1 tsp. grated Gruyère cheese (optional)
4 watercress leaves
1 tsp. fresh dill snips
2 tbsp. parsley
1 tbsp. chives

Chop herbs together very, very fine until you have reduced them to about 1½ tbsp. Use feathery part of dill. Put cream cheese into a bowl and press a garlic clove into it. Do not chop garlic as the pieces will be too large. Add enough oil to moisten. Mix in the grated Gruyère. Mix in the herbs and pack mixture into a crock and cover. Let stand in refrigerator for several hours to ripen. This cheese keeps up to two weeks and I use it as a stuffing for raw mushroom caps, to spread on cucumber or zucchini sticks or to tuck into radish rose petals or to fill celery sticks.

EVERYTHING IS popping now, and after the firecrackers are over, the garden keeps on going, each day bringing new fruits and vegetables. Your garden is entering the season of abundance and soon will be at its peak of production. If you've mulched well and kept a daily check on maverick weed progress, it is your happy duty just to pick. And pick you must, if you want the plants to keep bearing.

You can still replant lettuce, carrots, beets, and beans in short rows every two or three weeks. Pull the pea vines. Now you have quite a bit of extra space and you could put in fall cabbages and turnips where the peas came out. Or, depending on your own frost schedule (and it's always worth a gamble), the end of July could include a last planting of Romaine, two more rows of peas, and another row of beans.

Watch those beans. Once they start, there will be no stopping them—unless the Mexican bean beetle finds your garden. If you don't happen to spot the tiny fuzzy yellow bug on the underside of your bean leaves, the next sign will be lacy leaves. Then I would suggest a good dusting of Rotenone, and the same medicine goes for the potato beetle.

Other garden pests may start showing their unfriendly faces about now. There is one that

I find intriguing and am reluctant to destroy, although he doesn't feel that way about my parsley. If, one day, you are startled by a technicolor worm, wearing gold, green and black stripes and a Walt Disney-inspired face, you have just met the parsley worm. He likes carrot tops too. Just pick him off. He will leave agreeably.

I can't claim to be an authority on destructive garden insects because we have had very few, perhaps because our soil is extraordinarily healthy and we have always added compost, fertilizer, and mulch to it each year. We just have not found it necessary to use anything stronger than organic sprays on either orchard or vegetable garden.

Probably the most despised pest in the garden is the slug. It is one of those things, like the tick, that does not seem to have any reason for being. Dampness brings the slug, which is closely related to the snail. A dose of salt will eliminate it, and there is another method of dissolution, devised by Ruth Stout, that works amazingly well. Place saucers of beer strategically in your garden. In the morning you will find them full of dead slugs. If it doesn't take away your appetite for beer completely, it is a good way to get rid of them.

When you realize that the tomato plant can have thirty different pests and problems, it is a wonder that we ever have any. But obviously this is one of the bumper mid-summer crops all over the country, so the problem is not too difficult to cope with.

The one important fact to remember is to catch destructive insects early so they don't get too far along. Then you won't have to spray too close to the time the fruit is forming.

Everything "is the berries" right now and we become saturated with fruit cobblers, pies, slumps, pudding and fools. Jams and jellies must be made, especially the kinds you do not see on the supermarket shelves. As a hungry child very nicely put it, "Homemade jam has so much more in it, and it's runnier, too." I do like the looks of a pantry shelf with rows of deep red and purple jars, and if it is there it is amazing how often you will find uses for your homemade stores. A lovely jar of "runny" strawberry jam always suggests making popovers, for it deserves more than just toast. Blackberry or raspberry jam-filled pancakes are truly elegant for Sunday brunch or as a last-minute dessert, while blackberry jam as a filling for a plain white layer cake or a torte raises them to heavenly heights.

There is nothing quite like the flavor of wild fruits. The small low-bush blueberry that grows near the coast of Maine and in the woods of upper New England, as well as in the upper Great Lakes area, has a quality of tartness that is quite unlike cultivated berries. Unfortunately, we cannot easily transplant these bushes. So we are content with our Ivanhoes and Atlantics and make blueberry jam with a touch of cinnamon and lemon to add a wild flavor.

Blueberry Jam

2 quarts ripe blueberries
3 cups sugar
1 tbsp. lemon juice
1 inch stick cinnamon

Wash berries and place in large pan. Crush about 1/4 of the berries. Boil rapidly, stirring constantly for 5 minutes. Remove from heat. Add sugar, lemon juice and cinnamon. Boil rapidly with constant stirring and cook until thick and syrupy. Remove from heat. Pour into clean jars. Seal.

Blueberry pancakes are a must for Sunday morning breakfast with sausages and real maple syrup. Even the dieters break down and eat them. If you live near a watering spot, be it salt water or fresh, have a breakfast picnic some bright blue July morning and make blueberry pancakes on a griddle over charcoal or a wood fire. You may eat more than you should, but a long swim will have justified your appetite. Blueberry Upside Down Cake is so easy a child can make and enjoy it, and again it is a perfect dessert for a picnic because it transports easily.

An old favorite in our house is a pudding, served at the height of the blueberry season, always warm, always with ice cream. It is complete indulgence—no, immersion—in the beautiful blueberry.

July

Blueberry Upside Down Cake

      4 tbsp. butter
    ½ cup sugar
      1 egg
      1 tsp. vanilla
   1¼ cups flour
      2 tsp. baking powder
    ¼ tsp. salt
    ½ cup milk
      1 tbsp. butter
      1 cup sugar
      2 cups blueberries

Measure flour without sifting. Add to it the baking powder and salt. Cream butter with ½ cup sugar until light. Add egg, vanilla. Beat in flour mixture and milk alternately. Melt 1 tbsp. butter in 8-inch frying pan over low heat. Add 1 cup sugar and a few crushed blueberries. Stir until sugar is dissolved, add remaining berries. Pour cake batter on top and place in pre-heated 325° oven. Bake about 40 minutes, until cake tests done. Turn cake upside down on plate and serve warm with sweetened, lightly whipped cream.

Aunt Bet's Blueberry Pudding

      3 cups blueberries
    ⅔ cup sugar
      1 tsp. ground cinnamon
        juice of 1 lemon
    ⅔ cup flour
    ¼ cup butter

Place berries in buttered baking dish. Pour over berries ⅓ cup sugar. Sprinkle with cinnamon and lemon juice. Blend together the remaining ⅓ cup sugar, flour and butter until it becomes a crumbly mixture. Sprinkle it over berries. Bake at 350° for 40 minutes. Serve hot or cold.

July

BLACKBERRIES

For sheer beauty in the springtime, the blackberry flower is outstanding. If you've ever seen hedgerows of them, you might be inspired, as we were, to plant them on your property. We are interested in the eating possibilities as well—in deep-dish blackberry pies that have a crumbly sugary crust and ooze sweet, deep purple juice. Blackberries can be used for muffins and slumps and jam and jelly. They are quite seedy, so I advise straining out about half the seeds as for other berry jams. They also combine very well with red raspberries or currants.

Old-fashioned berry cordials still are a safe home remedy for what ails you. Blackberry is one of the few stringent fruits and is said to contain iron and be a generally effective tonic for the system. A little blackberry cordial is definitely not hard to take for a sore throat or cough; the official dosage is "from one teaspoonful to one wineglassful."

Blackberry Cordial

To three pounds uncooked berries add one pound white sugar and let stand twelve hours. Then press and strain, adding one-third rum or brandy and allowing one teaspoon powdered allspice to each quart of cordial. It must be bottled some time before it's fit for use.

Deep Dish Blackberry Pie

      4 cups blackberries
1½ cups sugar
      3 tbsp. flour
      1 tsp. grated orange rind
      1 recipe short pastry
      2 tbsp. butter

Place berries in fairly deep baking dish. Mix together the sugar, flour and orange rind. Toss berries in this mixture. Dot with butter. Cover with pastry crust rolled ¼ inch thick. Sprinkle heavily with sugar. Bake at 400° for 40 minutes. Serve with cream.

July

CHERRIES

Instead of a chicken in every pot, perhaps a future presidential candidate might introduce the idea of a cherry tree for every back yard, for every young American must know that story of the father of his country. But does anyone know exactly what kind of cherry tree it was?

Unfortunately, any fruiting cherry tree that is cut down today is sadly missed—just one more reason to plant at least three of your own. You can mix the sweet and sour and in that way have the best of two culinary worlds, with pies and cobblers from the bright pink, sour cherries, and cake and Cherry Bounce from the dark, sweet kind. I've read somewhere that cherries have the power to clear up certain kinds of depression, perhaps because they can be distilled into various kinds of alcoholic beverages without too much trouble. German kirschwasser, made from the fruit, is a very nice liqueur in which to bathe fruit such as strawberries. We all know the maraschino as a sticky sweet cherry in the bottom of a cocktail glass, but it also can be used to make a dessert jelly or a very rich concoction called Crème de Maraschino.

Next to George Washington, however, the person who comes first to mind is "Billy Boy" whose sweetheart could bake a cherry pie in the "twinkling of an eye." The mundane details of pitting the cherries obviously were not considered by that young lady. You will have to contend with them, though, so my advice is to buy a cherry pitter. It saves a lot of anguish and is handy also for pitting black cherries for a fruit salad.

A rosy red cherry pie bursting with tart-sweet juice and served warm is wonderful for breakfast, lunch, or dinner. At breakfast I would have just a glass of cold milk with it; for lunch, a bowl of fresh pea soup; and for dinner, a mustardy cheese soufflé with some thin-sliced ham and asparagus vinaigrette.

July

Sour Cherry Pie

4 cups sour cherries, pitted
1 cup sugar
4 tbsp. flour
   pastry for 2-crust 9-inch pie
¼ cup ground almonds

Toss cherries in bowl with sugar and flour. Line 9-inch pie pan with pastry. Chill for 15 minutes. Preheat oven to 425°. Bake pie shell for 10 minutes. Cool. Sprinkle ground almonds over bottom crust. Fill with cherries. Cover with pastry. Brush top crust with cream or egg white. Sprinkle with a little sugar. Bake at 400° for 40 minutes. Serve warm.

If you have an especially good crop of the tart cherries, and I hope you do, there is a spice-flavored cherry cake that stays moist a long time; and also a charming recipe from England called Aylesbury Cherry Bumpers, which are somewhat like closed-up tarts.

Sour Cherry Cake

½ cup butter
1 cup sugar
2 eggs
1¼ cups flour
2 tsp. baking powder
½ tsp. salt
1 tsp. cinnamon
½ tsp. soda
½ tsp. nutmeg
½ cup milk
2 cups sour cherries, pitted

Cream together the butter and sugar until light. Beat in eggs, one at a time. Combine flour, baking powder, salt, cinnamon and nutmeg, and soda. Add alternately to butter mixture with milk. Stir until smooth and creamy. Fold in cherries. Pour batter into 9-inch square pan. Bake at 350° for 30-35 minutes until cake tests done. When cool sprinkle with powdered sugar.

July

Aylesbury Cherry Bumpers

Pastry: 2 cups flour
         2 sticks butter
         6 tbsp. sour cream

Put all ingredients in bowl. Mix with fingers or pastry fork until a sticky ball is formed. Refrigerate for ½ hour.

Filling: 2 cups sour cherries, pitted
        ½ cup sugar
        ½ tsp. almond extract

Stew cherries with sugar until soft. Stir in almond extract. Roll the pastry to an ⅛-inch thickness. Cut into rounds about 5 inches in diameter, using a plate for a measure. Strain cherries from syrup. Place about 5 cherries in the middle of each round. Brush edges with unbeaten egg white. Fold each round in half and seal the edges firmly. Flute edges with tines of fork. Place on greased baking sheet. Brush with cherry syrup, sprinkle with sugar. Bake at 425° for 10 minutes until golden brown.

The sweet cherry is handsomer than the tart to look at and entirely different in flavor. It can be served as a dessert with no apologies if you also offer a soft cheese, such as a Danish Havarti, and a glass of white wine. Or these cherries can be incorporated into a Clafoutis, a type of flan which is founded on the sweet dark cherry cooked in a batter. It is worthwhile, too, just once, to try making Cherry Bounce. I have adapted an old recipe, and there is no doubt: it certainly does have bounce. It is not for children, but what a resounding dessert sauce at Thanksgiving!

July

Clafoutis

3 cups pitted sweet black cherries
2 tsp. lemon juice
3 tbsp. Kirsch
½ cup butter
½ cup sugar
1 tsp. lemon peel
¼ tsp. nutmeg
3 eggs
1 cup flour
1 tbsp. sugar

Put cherries, lemon juice, Kirsch in bowl and let stand 30 minutes. Cream butter with sugar, lemon and nutmeg. Beat in eggs. Mix in flour. Spread in greased, floured 9 or 10-inch spring form pan. Lift cherries from juice and put over batter. Mix 1 tbsp. sugar with juice and dribble over. Bake at 375° for 40 minutes. Let cool. Warm slightly before serving.

Cherry Bounce

4 pints cherries
1 quart rum or brandy
sugar to taste

Mash cherries and crack the stones. Put in a crock and pour rum or brandy over them. Let stand 10 days, stirring daily. Strain through several layers of cheesecloth lining a fine sieve. Sweeten to taste. Bottle.

Like all other berries and fruits, cherries (the sweet ones) make excellent jam, jelly, and conserve. Here is a recipe for a thick, fruity type of relish made with cherries, currant jelly and Port wine that will point up the flavors of an autumn game dinner.

Black Cherry Relish

2 6-oz. jars currant jelly
½ lb. sweet cherries, pitted
1 cup Port wine
½ cup sugar, or to taste
1 tbsp. lemon juice

Heat wine and sugar together, stirring, until sugar is dissolved. Add cherries and cook until fruit is soft but still whole. Add jelly and cook until syrupy. Stir in lemon juice. Pour into jars or glasses and cool. Keep in refrigerator.

RASPBERRIES

There are some foods each of us cares about more than anything else. There have to be favorites, or, as a wise man said, "All ice cream should be vanilla." Of all the fruits we grow, I really think that the raspberry is *my* favorite. It is such a perishable fruit and the season is so comparatively short, I haunt the raspberry patch, reluctant to let one berry go beyond its prime. They must be eaten on the spot, for even a few hours on the counter reduces their flavor greatly.

I have memories of one wonderfully indulgent morning as a child when I was allowed to eat as many pieces as I could manage of toasted homemade bread liberally spread with fresh raspberry jam. The number eight sticks in my mind.

Now, I'm sorry to say, we ration the amount of jam used at one sitting, because our patch's production is limited. There has to be one batch of raspberry muffins from it, however, and perhaps one raspberry shortcake. But the greatest treat of all is to walk through the raspberry patch with cereal bowl in hand and fill it with the deep red tart berries which take so kindly to a sprinkling of superfine sugar and a bit of heavy cream.

Raspberry Muffins

2 cups flour + 2 tbsp.
⅓ cup sugar
2 tsp. baking powder
½ tsp. salt
2 eggs
¾ cup milk
3 tbsp. melted butter
1½ cups raspberries

Put dry ingredients in bowl. Add, and quickly stir in, the eggs, milk and melted butter. Fold in raspberries. Fill buttered muffin cups. Sprinkle tops with sugar. Bake at 400° for 15 minutes.

Perhaps it is unfair to rhapsodize over the wild fruits, when our suburban areas have so few of them. But there is one kind that is found as far south as Virginia and north to our part of Connecticut in many fields that have been left uncultivated. We discovered it almost in our backyard by chance one sum-

mer morning when the rest of our berries were over and done with. It seemed to have sprung full-grown from nowhere, although Euall Gibbons writes that it is a recent immigrant from Asia, now thoroughly naturalized.

Gibbons identifies it as the Wineberry, a relative of the raspberry. It has long canes that re-root themselves at the tips and which are very bristly and prickly. Gathering them is more of a chore than picking cultivated raspberries, but well worth the scratches. The berry is brighter red than its cousin and slightly sticky to the touch.

Gibbons says that in spite of the name, he has never heard of anyone making wine from wineberries. But we have combined them with currants and made the most beautiful ruby red jelly to use as a glaze for fruit tarts, as a sauce for chicken or game when combined with Port wine and orange rind, and to serve just plain with wild duck or pheasant. If you have a bumper crop of these berries, too much to make into jelly, just freeze the strained juice and make jelly later when the kitchen is cooler.

Currant and Wineberry Jelly

3 cups currants
3 cups wineberries
½ cup water
  sugar

Wash and stem currants. Put currants and wineberries in pan with ½ cup water. Bring to a boil and boil 10 minutes. Put mixture into jelly bag and let drip over bowl without squeezing. Measure juice into saucepan. Add equal amount of sugar. Cook, stirring, until sugar dissolves. Boil for 6 or 7 minutes until juice sheets from spoon. Pour into jelly glasses. Seal with wax.

July

BROCCOLI

July being the busy month it is in the garden, we jump from one thing to another like the grasshopper, tasting a bit of this, a lot of that, relishing anew the flavors of summer. We pick tender new green beans only 3 inches long, just right for a salad. We cut the tiny flowerets of broccoli, a vegetable that must be picked very young (when the heads are about a quarter the size of the market variety) and picked very often so that it won't flower. Cut the broccoli two to four inches below the head and refrigerate immediately, for it is very perishable.

Luckily, there are many good things to do with broccoli, and your six plants will be used without waste or much left for the neighbors. It is a very nutritious vegetable and makes delicious soup, salad, and soufflé, and it lends itself to both hot and cold service. When you pick your own broccoli, the stalks will be tender and not need peeling. If any stalks are over a half inch in diameter, you can split them. Like asparagus, the broccoli head and stalk must be cooked to the same degree of doneness. Be sure to soak the heads in salt water for half an hour, as there's bound to be at least one small green worm waving its antennae at you.

I recommend cooking it the way I cook green beans: for a very short time in a large amount of water. After five minutes of boiling, test by sticking the point of a knife into the stem. If barely tender, drain and cool immediately. This is enough cooking for use in a salad with a sharp dressing and a garnish of radishes. It is enough when made into soup or chopped for a soufflé or combined with the Italian seasonings of oil and garlic, with anchovy and white wine for an authoritative vegetable dish.

July

Cold Broccoli Soup

1 lb. broccoli
2 scallions, chopped
2 stalks celery and leaves, chopped
4 cups chicken broth
2 tbsp. butter
1 tbsp. flour
1 tsp. salt
  dash of Tabasco
1 cup light cream
2 tbsp. each chopped chives and parsley

Melt butter in saucepan. Sauté scallion and celery until soft. Cut flowerets off broccoli and cut up stems. Sprinkle flour over scallions and cook for 1 minute. Pour in chicken broth. Add cut-up broccoli. Simmer until vegetables are tender. Add salt and Tabasco. Put soup into blender and blend until smooth. Chill. Before serving, add cream and sprinkle with chives and parsley.

Marinated Broccoli

1 lb. broccoli
½ cup chicken broth
2 hardboiled egg yolks
1 tsp. salt
3 tbsp. oil
  freshly ground pepper
1 tsp. sugar
½ tsp. grated onion
2 tbsp. herb vinegar

Cook broccoli until just tender. Drain and dry. Mash egg yolks with salt and oil. With fork, blend in pepper, sugar, onion and vinegar. Make a smooth mixture. Whip in chicken broth. Pour over broccoli and chill. Garnish with chopped radishes.

Broccoli Soufflé

1 cup cooked, chopped broccoli
3 tbsp. butter
3 tbsp. flour
1 cup milk
1 tsp. salt
¼ tsp. pepper
1 tsp. Worcestershire sauce
5 egg yolks
6 egg whites
½ cup grated Parmesan cheese

Melt butter in saucepan. Add flour and cook, stirring, until golden and bubbly. Add milk, all at once, and cook, stirring, over high heat until thick and smooth. Remove from heat. Add salt, pepper, and Worcestershire. Add egg yolks, one at a time. Stir in chopped broccoli. Beat whites until stiff but not dry. Fold into broccoli mixture. Pour into soufflé dish. Sprinkle with ¼ cup grated Parmesan cheese. Bake at 350° for 30-35 minutes. Serve immediately.

To prepare soufflé dish: butter a 1½ quart straight-sided baking dish. Sprinkle with ¼ cup grated Parmesan over bottom of dish.

Roman Broccoli

1 bunch broccoli
3 tbsp. olive oil
1 garlic clove, mashed
1 anchovy, mashed
½ tsp. salt
½ tsp. pepper
1½ cups dry red wine

Cut broccoli into small flowerets. Heat oil in skillet and add garlic clove and anchovy. Cook briefly. Do not let garlic burn. Add broccoli, salt and pepper. Cook, stirring, for 5 minutes. Add wine and cover pan. Cook for 10 minutes until vegetable is tender, over very low heat.

Reversing somewhat my former stand on puréed vegetables, I *do* like puréed broccoli because it will not become too smooth, due to the stems—and there are many uses for it. Try puréed broccoli masked with an oniony cream sauce when you are having a piece of beef or lamb. Sprinkle some grated cheese on top and run it under the broiler just before serving. Or use puréed broccoli as a base for plain, boned, poached chicken breasts all arranged carefully on a round platter with Hollandaise

covering the whole thing. There is lovely color to this dish. A simple but attractive luncheon menu can be worked around a casserole of puréed broccoli or spinach mixed with a Mornay sauce on which you have placed stuffed hard-boiled eggs with more sauce poured over the eggs.

BEANS

It stands to reason that you like green beans. They are so basic a vegetable that even children won't quarrel with it. Planting a ten-foot row of beans every three weeks will keep you well, but not overwhelmingly, supplied with beans for the summer.

There is a simple method of cooking beans so that they will keep their color and their shape. We have all finally learned that there is nothing to be said for the boil-to-death manner of cooking that produced gray, limp strings destined for a watery grave from the moment they were plucked from the bush.

And the addition of soda was no improvement.

To cook green or wax beans: Top and tail beans. Put a large saucepan of water on high heat (3 quarts of water for 1 lb. of beans). When water is boiling hard, add 1 tsp. salt. Put in beans and boil, uncovered, for 3 minutes. Test bean. If it is tender crisp, they are done. Large beans will take a bit longer. Drain into colander and run beans under cold water until cool. Place on towel to dry. At this point, the beans can be held in the refrigerator until the next day if necessary. To

serve: Heat 1 tbsp. oil in large frying pan. Put in beans and stir around rapidly to get off all excess moisture. Add 6 tbsp. butter in pieces, stirring over high heat. When hot, put in serving dish and sprinkle with parsley.

At first, pick your beans very small and enjoy them dressed simply with butter, salt, pepper and a bit of nutmeg. Then, as they get larger or to vary the routine, you can flavor them with oil and garlic or shallots, a little tomato, parsley, chives or savory, or serve them en casserole with a creamy mushroom sauce or a light Béchamel. None of us likes "beany" beans, but when the vines are almost through we do find large beans hiding underneath the foliage. Though somewhat larger than we like, they are still fresh and tasty and are delicious in soup. A very good dish is called Snibbled Beans from Pennsylvania Dutch country.

Incidentally, string beans are no longer thus. How long has it been since you strung a bean or needed to? That went out with overcooking. The proper name is now "snap" bean and that they should do, with an audible sound.

July

Snibbled Beans

1 lb. green beans in ½-inch pieces
2 slices bacon, diced
2 potatoes, diced in ½-inch pieces
1 large tomato, peeled, chopped
¼ cup chicken broth
    freshly ground pepper

Cook diced bacon in frying pan until crisp. Remove bacon. Add potatoes and stir until lightly browned. Add green beans, tomato and chicken broth. Cover and cook until vegetables are tender. Sprinkle with diced bacon and freshly ground pepper before serving. Salt to taste.

Green Beans Nicoise

½ cup olive oil
2 shallots minced
½ garlic clove, minced
2 tomatoes, peeled and chopped
½ cup celery chopped
1 tsp. salt
    freshly ground pepper
1 tsp. minced fresh oregano
1 tsp. minced fresh basil
1 lb. green beans, cooked until just tender
1 tbsp. chopped parsely

Heat oil. Add shallots and garlic and cook until limp. Add tomatoes, celery, salt, pepper, and chicken broth. Simmer, uncovered, about 20 minutes. Stir in herbs and beans. Simmer until beans are hot.

July

Italian Green Beans

1 lb. green beans cooked until just tender
1 garlic clove, minced
2 tomatoes, peeled and chopped
½ cup diced ham
¼ cup grated Parmesan cheese
2 tbsp. olive oil
1 tsp. grated black pepper
1 tsp. salt

Cover bottom of small frying pan with olive oil. Add garlic. Sauté briefly. Add tomatoes, ham, salt, pepper and beans. Simmer for about 10 minutes until tomatoes have given up some of their moisture Sprinkle grated Parmesan cheese over top and serve.

Cooked briefly, the small, whole, very green beans are ready for salads; to combine with shrimps or tuna fish in an oil and lemon juice dressing; or used with thinly sliced raw mushrooms, diced cucumbers and a little chopped garlic in a simple French dressing. Or, arrange the small cooked beans on a platter and cover with chopped red radishes. Just before serving, sprinkle with fresh lemon juice, salt, and ground black pepper.

Dill goes well with green beans, and a summery main dish for a cool night might be created by browning 2 lbs. of stewing veal in butter and oil, seasoning well with paprika, salt, and pepper, and simmering until tender (about 1¼ hours) in chicken broth to cover. Half an hour before serving, add ½ cup diced raw potatoes and the same quantity of cut-up scallions. Then in 15 minutes put in 2 full handfuls of raw green beans cut into 1-inch pieces and a tbsp. of snipped dill. Let this simmer together until the vegetables are tender and the aromatic flavors have increased your appetite twofold. When you can't wait a minute longer, serve your feast garnished with more dill. If you like a creamier sauce, stir in a cup of sour cream to which you add a tbsp. of flour.

A slightly different sauce (and that's what we are looking for by August) is made by browning chopped walnuts in butter, adding the cooked beans and warming them through.

Or try sour cream warmed with chopped tarragon and paprika.

Wax beans can be used in many of the ways that you use green beans. I no longer plant them because they just don't generate enough family excitement to justify the garden space. If you have them, though, you might try a sweet and sour recipe that perks them up considerably.

Sweet and Sour Wax Beans

1 lb. wax beans, cut up
1 small onion, sliced
2 tsp. salt
½ cup water
½ cup vinegar
4 tbsp. sugar
2 tbsp. butter

Combine vinegar, water, sugar and salt in saucepan. Heat until sugar dissolves. Add onion and wax beans. Cover and simmer until beans are crisp tender. Add butter and serve.

SQUASHES

There are squashes and squashes, and no matter how you figured it on your garden plan, you are liable to have more than you bargained for. However, squashes can be used at almost any size except for the "brickbats" which are best in the compost heap. Waste-not-want-not is one of the best adages to apply to the garden. The more we put in, certainly the more we get out. Like any of your vegetables, squash are most tender and moist when used shortly after picking. This is especially true of the overlarge ones which can be used stuffed with innumerable combinations of things. They lose their good qualities in a day and, to my way of thinking, they become perfect examples of what the British call "marrows."

Zucchini and yellow squash (also known as summer or crookneck) contain a lot of water and therefore should not be immersed in water for cooking. Home-grown squash does not need to be peeled unless, for some reason, it develops a particularly bumpy skin, which occasionally happens to the yellow type. It doesn't affect the flavor although the appearance makes you wonder if you've grown a new variety of gourd. The disposal of seeds in squash is optional. The squash is related to the cucumber, and do you eat cucumber seeds? I do in the summer. I don't in the winter. Right out of the garden they are not noticeable.

Of all of the summer squashes, the yellow has the mildest flavor, so you may feel a bit heavier hand on the seasoning is needed. A lot of salt, pepper, shallots, onion, parsley, chives, dill, savory or marjoram can be used to good advantage. I reserve the garlic for the zucchini, for somehow it goes better there.

Simple Summer Squash

2 lbs. yellow squash
  water
2 chopped shallots
1 tsp. salt
  freshly ground black pepper

Cut up the squash in rounds, about ¼ inch wide. Put into saucepan with chopped shallots, salt, and one inch of water. Cover and steam until tender. Use a large pan so that squash will all be done at the same time. Serve with butter and lots of pepper.

July

Yellow Squash en Casserole

2 lbs. yellow squash
2 tsp. salt
½ cup bread crumbs
3 eggs
1 cup sour cream
½ cup grated Cheddar cheese
1 tsp. paprika
½ tsp. thyme
1 tbsp. chopped parsley
2 tbsp. melted butter

Grate squash. Mix with salt and let stand 30 minutes. Press out all liquid. Mix squash with bread crumbs, eggs, sour cream, cheese, paprika, thyme, parsley, and pour into buttered baking dish. Pour melted butter over top. Bake at 350° for 50 minutes until set and golden.

Tiny Stuffed Squash

6 yellow squash 4 inches long
4 medium-sized carrots
4 tsp. butter
1 tsp. salt
cream
½ tsp. nutmeg
1 tbsp. chopped chives

Parboil squash until just tender. Drain and cool. Cut in half and hollow out centers. Meanwhile, cut up carrots and cook until soft. Purée in blender with salt, melted butter, and enough cream to moisten. Beat in nutmeg. Fill squashes with carrot mixture. Sprinkle with chopped chives and place in oven to warm through.

July

Yellow Squash Sauté

2 lbs. yellow squash
2 tsp. salt
2 tbsp. butter
1 tbsp. grated onion
1 cup cream
    grated rind of 1 lemon
½ tsp. pepper

Cut squash into thin strips. Mix with salt in bowl and let stand for 30 minutes. Drain and press moisture out of squash. Melt butter in large frying pan. Add pepper, onion and squash. Simmer, uncovered, 10 minutes. Pour in cream and increase heat, letting mixture bubble until slightly thickened. Stir in lemon rind. Serve very hot.

My own favorite, I must admit, is the variegated long green squash known as zucchini in this country and as courgette abroad. We never seem to grow too much of it, or perhaps we have friends who like it as much as we do. One in particular, who spends a lot of time boating, has her standard lunch centered around large amounts of cold zucchini soup which she whips up at home and takes aboard. Should I say that even teen-agers like it? Or are you of the mind that this particular age group will not eat anything that is noticeably good for them? Here is one thing that is very good for them *and* they love it.

According to a well-known nutritionist, zucchini is among our best all-purpose natural foods, and when it is picked three inches long, sun-warmed and buttery to the taste and touch, and eaten raw right in the garden, one can feel good health emanating from every pore. But that is all part of summer. It should be the time when we are building ourselves up mentally and physically to draw on in the leaner months ahead.

July

Grated Squash

4 summer squash
4 tbsp. butter
1 medium onion
1 tsp. salt
   freshly ground black pepper
2 tbsp. chopped parsley

Shred unpeeled squash on large hole grater.
Grate onion. Put butter, vegetables in large
frying pan with seasonings. Cover and place
on high heat. Cook about 5 minutes. Uncover
and cook over high heat to evaporate liquid.
Serve immediately.

Zucchini Hors d'Oeuvres

4 tbsp. butter
1 tsp. minced parsley
1 clove garlic
1 small shallot
2 medium zucchinis
   paprika

Soften butter and blend it well with parsley,
mashed garlic, and minced shallot. Slice unpeeled zucchinis into rounds and spread with
butter. Sprinkle lightly with paprika. Place
rounds on baking sheet and bake at 500° for
6-8 minutes. Serve hot.

July

Zucchini Soup

3 medium zucchinis
1 medium onion
4 stalks celery with leaves
3 tbsp. butter
6 cups chicken broth
1 tsp. salt
   freshly ground pepper
1 tsp. chopped fresh tarragon

Cut unpeeled zucchini into thin slices. Dice celery. Slice onion into thin rings. Melt butter in large pan. Sauté celery and onion slowly until limp. Add zucchini slices and sauté for 5 minutes. Add chicken broth, cover, and simmer until vegetables are soft. Put into blender with pepper, salt, and tarragon. Blend until smooth. Chill. Before serving, add 1 cup light cream or rich milk.

We still turn to Europe for imaginative ways to cook certain vegetables and, in the case of zucchini, Italy is an important source of inspiration. They have a simple marinated zucchini that makes good use of their extra-large and juicy lemons. It is excellent for a summer buffet along with a poached salmon or bass or a roast chicken tarragon and with cold rice that has been marinated in French dressing and mixed with a lot of chopped cucumber, chives, and parsley.

Marinated Zucchini

3 medium zucchinis
2 tbsp. oil
   freshly ground black pepper
   juice of 1 large lemon

Slice zucchini into ¼-inch rounds. Poach briefly in a small amount of boiling salted water until just tender, about 3 minutes. Drain and dry on paper towels. Place rounds on flat serving dish; do not layer. Pour oil over all and lots of black pepper. Let stand at room temperature. Just before serving, squeeze fresh lemon juice over all.

Parmesan cheese and garlic help to create another plain but good recipe that gives full appreciation to small, small zucchinis. Anchovy, an interesting flavor that we tend to forget about, combines nicely with other ingredients to make stuffed zucchinis a good main dish supper. And just for fun, and to keep your family coming back for more, you might serve a platter of stuffed vegetables, including squash, tomatoes, onions, and peppers. This will provide a good variety of color, shape and texture. The only accompaniment needed is some Arab bread and a fruit dessert.

Broiled Baby Zucchinis

Pick zucchinis 3-4 inches long. Split the long way. Place on a broiler tray and spread with butter. Sprinkle with chopped garlic and grated Parmesan cheese, a little salt and pepper. Broil about 4 inches from flame until bubbling.

Stuffed Zucchinis

3 larger zucchinis
   olive oil
½ cup cooked rice or wheat pilaf
2 garlic cloves, mashed
¼ cup chopped pine nuts or walnuts
2 tbsp. chopped parsley
3 anchovy fillets, chopped
1 egg

Parboil zucchinis 5-10 minutes until tender. Cut in half lengthwise and scoop out seeds and a small amount of flesh. Sauté garlic in oil. Add nuts, rice, parsley, anchovies and egg. Cook, stirring, until well mixed. Stuff zucchinis with mixture. Arrange in baking dish. Brush with oil. Bake at 375° for 20 minutes. Serve lukewarm.

Moving a little farther east in our geography, we can take a typically Mid-Eastern dish called Moussaka and adapt it to the seasonal produce of our gardens. Traditionally made with eggplant, lamb, and a somewhat custardy sauce, it works very well with a minimum of meat, a maximum of zucchini and tomato sauce—another good item for the summer buffet table.

Zucchini Moussaka

3 lbs. small zucchinis
1 lb. ground lamb
4 lbs. tomatoes, skinned, chopped
3 large onions, chopped
3 garlic cloves, crushed
2/3 cup bread crumbs
4 eggs
   olive oil
   salt and pepper
3 tsp. ground allspice
1 tbsp. chopped mint
   chicken or beef stock

Wash zucchini but do not peel. Cut lengthwise into 1/8-inch slices. Sprinkle with salt and leave in colander with weight on top for 1 hour. (A plate with a heavy can on it will do for a weight.) Dry zucchini slices on paper towels. Sauté lightly and quickly in oil. Remove. Add more oil and sauté onion until tender. Put in meat and brown. Add salt and pepper to taste, allspice and mint. Stir in eggs. In separate saucepan put skinned and chopped tomatoes with crushed garlic. Simmer until most of moisture is evaporated. Oil a 2-qt. flat baking dish. Put in a layer of zucchini, a layer of meat, a layer of tomatoes. Repeat, finishing with tomatoes. Sprinkle with bread crumbs. Moisten with stock. Cover with foil. Bake for 1 hour at 325°. Remove foil. Bake for 1 hour more.

Don't forget to use zucchini spears for hors d'oeuvres either to dip into curried mayonnaise or to spread with an herbed cheese. They also are tasty fried in oil lightly and marinated in a dressing of 2 parts vinegar to 1 part oil, minced garlic, chopped basil, parsley, salt and pepper. And to give the Italians full credit, they offer a superb sauce for pasta with zucchini as the main ingredient.

July

Zucchini Sauce for Pasta

3 small zucchinis
1 fresh tomato
2 tbsp. oil
2 tbsp. butter
1 tsp. salt
  freshly ground pepper
½ cup grated Parmesan cheese
½ lb. thin spaghetti

Cut zucchinis into small rounds. Peel and chop tomato. Heat oil and butter together. Sauté zucchini briefly. Add tomato and cook for 10 minutes until blended. Meanwhile, cook pasta in large amount of boiling salted water until just tender. Drain. Toss with 2 tbsp. butter and zucchini and tomato mixture. Sprinkle with pepper and grated cheese. Serve immediately.

There's another summer squash (a generalized term covering all squashes maturing in July and August) that is fairly new to the home gardener. It's the pattypan or white bush scallop. Its uses are not as varied as the zucchini or yellow, but it is fun to experiment with. If you can catch these squashes when they are tiny, they make a most unusual meal.

Sautéed Pattypan

Take medium-sized pattypan squash and slice across into flat slices. Sauté in butter until tender and lightly browned. Sprinkle with sugar and glaze briefly.

July

Stuffed Pattypan

½ lb. mushrooms
4 tbsp. butter
2 tbsp. flour
½ cup cream
12 very small pattypan squashes

Chop mushrooms very fine. Sauté in butter until they give up most of their moisture. Stir in flour. Cook briefly. Stir in cream. Add salt and pepper to taste. Parboil squashes until just tender. Cut off tops and hollow out insides. Fill with creamed mushrooms. Put tops back on. Serve hot.

Scalloped Pattypan

4 medum-sized pattypans
4 tbsp. butter
4 tbsp. flour
2 cups milk
1 tsp. salt
1 dash Tabasco
½ tsp. dry mustard
½ cup grated cheese mixed with
½ cup bread crumbs

Parboil squashes in boiling salted water until just tender. Cut into crosswise slices. Melt butter in saucepan. Stir in flour and cook until golden and bubbly. Pour in milk and cook until thick and smooth. Season with salt, Tabasco, and mustard. Layer squash slices and sauce in buttered baking dish. Sprinkle with cheese and crumbs. Reheat and run under broiler to brown.

July

TOMATOES

Though it was totally ignored in this country until the early 1800s, the tomato, or love apple, now would be voted the most popular, most useful, most revered vegetable—at least in July and August. To many people, summer is not really here until they have had their first ripe tomato.

Tomatoes surely are one of the most versatile fruits (and it *is* really that) we have. They can be eaten raw, stewed, baked, fried, broiled, in soups, stews, soufflés, pies, alone or with any number of other vegetables. There are so many ways of preparing this garden gem that I hesitate to embark on the subject for fear that I'll never get off it. I'll just give you a few of my favorite recipes, some of which may be familiar since they are strictly hand-me-downs that are pulled from my files every year about this time.

We do eat tomatoes for breakfast, lunch, and dinner. A superb and quickly-made breakfast is a version of an English grill with bacon, tomatoes, and chicken livers all cooked separately, albeit in the same pan. Fry your bacon slices first, putting them on paper towels in a warm oven. Next cook the livers in a small amount of the bacon fat with a little butter added. When they are done, add them to the platter warming in the oven. Add a bit of bacon fat and quickly fry the tomato slices which have been sprinkled with sugar, salt and pepper. When they are soft and slightly browned, take them out and deglaze your pan by adding a bit more butter and some lemon juice and swirling it all around quickly, scraping up the bits from the bottom of the pan. Pour over the tomato slices and chicken livers and sprinkle with minced parsley. Serve with English muffins and homemade strawberry jam.

A knowledgeable friend once told me that she never puts vinegar on her raw tomato slices; just oil and a tiny bit of sugar. She says that the tomatoes are acid enough. I have been doing this, and she is absolutely right. My only addition is a good sprinkling of

chopped basil, which truly is *the* tomato herb.

Cold tomatoes come into their own on hot summer nights, when there is nothing more attractive than a large platter of tomato slices surrounding another marinated vegetable such as cucumbers. But for a change try a spicier tomato slice or even some small stuffed tomatoes. I say small because I think that the larger fruits should be served as a separate course.

Piquant Tomato Slices

4 ripe tomatoes
2 tbsp. minced shallots
½ tsp. dried chili peppers
4 tbsp. oil
1 tsp. minced fresh ginger root
½ tsp. ground ginger
4 tbsp. grated fresh coconut
2 tbsp. chopped fresh mint

Do not peel tomatoes. Slice into ½-inch thick slices. Sauté shallots in oil until limp. Do not burn. Mix together the peppers, ginger and coconut. Dip each tomato slice into the mixture and sauté in pan until lightly brown. Chill. Sprinkle with mint before serving.

July

Cold Stuffed Tomatoes

6 ripe tomatoes
1 20-oz. can white kidney beans
1 garlic clove, crushed
1 tbsp. chopped parsley
1 tsp. salt
  freshly ground pepper
2 tbsp. herb vinegar
3 tbsp. oil

Put beans in sieve and run under cold water until thoroughly rinsed and water runs clear. Drain. Hollow out tomatoes and sprinkle insides with salt. Turn upside down to drain for 20 minutes. Put beans in bowl and add oil, vinegar, salt, garlic, lots of pepper and parsley. When tomatoes are drained, fill with beans. Chill. Let come to room temperature before serving.

This glorious fruit is a natural for soup, cold or hot, and it can be stuffed with any number of exciting things to make it the focal point of a luncheon or dinner menu. Try whole chicken livers that you have sautéed quickly in butter and sprinkled with lemon juice and a bit of chopped sage; or creamed shrimp subtly seasoned with dill; or artichoke hearts that have been marinated in French dressing and then smothered with a sour cream and mayonnaise sauce; or grilled mushrooms and herbed rice. When using tomatoes, the main question is: to peel or not to peel. I believe in peeling all tomatoes unless they are going to be stuffed or fried, when obviously they cannot hold their shapes without their skins. Who could? To peel them, plunge into boiling water for a count of 10, then immediately into cold water.

Of all of the vegetables that have been grown *out* of their natural seasons, I believe that tomatoes come off the worst. There has been quite a lot written about the tasteless tomato that we must put up with most of the year. That is why we so look forward to our own garden variety, to use in recipes that absolutely must have native vine-ripened tomatoes.

There is a soup that we just cannot serve too often, and we have it at least once a week during the season. It is a cold soup for hot nights or a hot soup for cool nights.

Tomato Cob

6 large tomatoes, peeled
½ medium onion, grated
1 tsp. salt
  freshly ground pepper
6 tbsp. mayonnaise
1 tsp. curry powder

Peel tomatoes by plunging them into boiling water. Chop peeled tomatoes into very small pieces and put them, with their juice, into a bowl. Grate onion into tomatoes. Stir in salt and pepper. Chill for at least 2 hours. Serve in individual soup bowls with a spoonful of mayonnaise mixed with curry powder on top. Note: show your guests the proper way to eat this soup, by mixing the mayonnaise into the tomatoes first.

Cream of Tomato

4 cups chopped fresh tomatoes
1 onion, chopped
4 whole cloves
6 peppercorns
1 tsp. brown sugar
1 tsp. salt
4 sprigs parsley
1½ cups chicken broth
1 cup heavy cream
3 tbsp. butter
3 tbsp. flour

Simmer tomatoes, onion, cloves, peppercorns, sugar, parsley, salt together 10 minutes. Put through food mill. Melt butter, add flour and stir until golden. Pour in chicken broth and stir until thickened. Add tomato mixture and cream and heat thoroughly.

The simplest thing in the world would seem to be a tomato sandwich. Unfortunately, it can be the *messiest* thing in the world, and while that is all right for the children (who seem to prefer sandwiches sodden with mayonnaise and slightly damp throughout), your ladies' luncheon, tea, or garden club group does not.

There *is* a way to make tomato sandwiches ahead of time and have them presentable at the crucial moment. The secret is in the slicing. Set the tomato on its stem end and slice it up and down, not crosswise. Then take out the wet seedy part, leaving just the flesh. Spread the bread with butter, not mayonnaise, and put the tomato slices on with salt and pepper. Cover with another thin slice of buttered bread and you have an unsoggy tomato sandwich.

This recipe comes from friend Nika Hazelton whose Italian cooking is *par excellence*.

Roman Tomatoes

8 medium-sized to large tomatoes
½ cup olive oil
⅓ cup chopped parsley
2 cloves garlic, minced
1 cup rice
2 cups hot chicken broth
  salt
  pepper
⅛ tsp. cinnamon

Cut slices from tops of tomatoes and scoop out center with a spoon. Save juice. Place tomatoes in shallow baking dish. Sprinkle each tomato with 1 tsp. oil. Heat remaining oil in saucepan. Cook garlic and parsley in it 3 minutes. Add rice and cook 3 minutes more, stirring constantly. Add hot chicken broth. Cover and cook 15 minutes, or until rice is three-quarters done. Remove from heat; season with salt and pepper and cinnamon. Fill tomatoes with rice mixture. Pour tomato juice over tomatoes to the depth of ½ inch up side of tomatoes. Bake uncovered at 350° for about 30 minutes until rice is tender but tomatoes are still holding their shape. Baste occasionally. Serve warm or at room temperature.

July

Wet Deviled Tomatoes

4 tbsp. softened butter
3 hard-cooked egg yolks
1 tsp. sugar
1 tsp. dry mustard
3 drops Tabasco
¼ cup tarragon vinegar
2 eggs
4 large tomatoes
  toast rounds spread with anchovy paste

Blend butter with hard-cooked egg yolks. Work in sugar, mustard, Tabasco. Heat the vinegar until hot but not boiling. Remove from the stove and stir into it the two raw eggs, beating until creamy. Mix this with the butter and egg yolks. The whole should be as thick as soft custard. Dip the tomatoes and slip off skins. Cut in inch-thick slices and put under broiler for 5 minutes. Place on toast rounds and pour over the sauce.

Cheese Fondue Tomatoes

6 large tomatoes
2 slices bread
¼ lb. Cheddar cheese
  butter
1 tsp. salt
  mustard
3 eggs
1½ cups milk
½ tsp. Worcestershire sauce
  paprika

Cut crusts off bread. Spread with butter and mustard. Cut into ½-inch cubes. Beat eggs in bowl with milk, salt, Worcestershire and paprika. Cut cheese into ½-inch cubes. Add bread and cheese cubes to egg mixture. Let stand 1 hour. Slice tops off tomatoes, take out insides and turn over to drain. Place tomatoes in shallow baking dish. Fill with cheese mixture. Bake at 350° for 35 minutes until set and puffed up. Serve hot.

July

Tomatoes Fried the Old-Fashioned Way

4 large tomatoes
flour
salt
pepper
heavy cream
bacon fat

Slice tomatoes into fairly thick slices. Dip in flour, salt and pepper. Heat bacon fat in frying pan. Fry tomato slices until brown and crusty on both sides. Remove to warm platter. Pour in heavy cream and bring to a boil scrapings from bottom of pan. Pour over tomatoes and serve with individual corn puddings.

Broiled Tomatoes

4 large tomatoes
2 garlic cloves
¼ cup white wine
½ cup olive oil
½ cup chopped parsley
1 tsp. salt
½ tsp. pepper

Cut tomatoes in halves. Place in buttered shallow baking dish. Place all other ingredients in blender and blend well. Pour over tomatoes. Broil until hot and bubbling.

Fried, baked, broiled, filled with cheese or rice, seasoned with herbs, garlic, anchovy, or deviled in a very special way that I remember from childhood, the tomato is all goodness; it's all the very soul of summer.

August

August

AUGUST'S GARDEN should be bursting at the seams. It is almost too much to cope with, but it is the best kind of surfeit—providing simple meals from the fruits of your labors. Cucumbers that don't have to be peeled or seeded; onions to flavor casseroles or to eat in plain or fancy dress; corn that we never seem to get enough of; limas that combine with corn in cream and butter; eggplant, the recognized beauty of the patch; and celery, cabbage and cauliflower—all are given their just due now.

The dog days are here, and the cicada's drone gives us the warning that it is six weeks until frost. That means no more planting unless a row of radishes or a few carrots and beets. It's just as well; we're too busy picking.

This is the month when no gardener wants to go away on vacation; perhaps we have a dog-in-the-manger attitude, for there always are well-meaning friends who will pick while we're gone. But will they pick the right things at the right time, and will they pick often enough? And will they leave anything for us when we arrive home, sated with too much hotel food and no fresh vegetables? No, it really is easier to get someone to care for the chickens and the cat than the garden. Let's postpone our visits until fall when the garden is under control and we have reaped its greatest rewards.

August

CELERY

The nice thing about growing your own celery is that you can pick it by the stalk. A little of it always is useful; but a whole bunch often is too much. Being able to pick a bit now and then may get you into the habit of using celery, which has a really distinctive flavor, instead of leaving it out of a recipe because you don't know what to do with the rest of the large bunch.

Celery sticks, raw or cooked, are an attractive garnish or a vegetable course in themselves, and the leaves add a great deal to many soups, stews, and sauces. Creamed celery has been spoiled for most of us because it was never done in an attractive manner. The celery was limp and, not being properly drained, the water leaked out into the cream sauce. It was all white and watery.

Actually, I don't think celery needs a sauce. It is much better just braised in butter or sprinkled with a few chopped almonds and some parsley. There's even such a thing as a celery soufflé which is made with the basic soufflé recipe using a cup of puréed celery. The celery first has been cooked until soft in chicken stock, with a little leek, parsley, mace, and bay leaf in the pan.

I always add some diced celery to a tomato sauce or stewed tomatoes, or to a combination of green beans and tomatoes. What I am saying is that you should use celery for itself, not just as an extender to make the chicken or shrimp go farther.

Braised Celery Sticks

Cut celery stalks into sticks 4 inches long and a quarter inch wide, allowing about 8 per person. Put in a saucepan with some of the leaves. Cover with water, 1 tsp. salt, and bring to a boil. Simmer for 8 minutes until celery is tender but still crisp. Drain on paper towels. Reduce liquid in pan to ¼ cup, swirl in a good pat of butter, and pour over celery sticks. Sprinkle with parsley.

Celery Amandine

Dice celery into 1-inch pieces. Place in sauce-pan with chicken or beef broth to cover. Cook until just tender. Drain. Melt butter in frying pan and sauté celery until lightly browned. Remove. Sauté slivered almonds (about 1 tbsp. to 1 cup celery) until browned. Toss nuts and celery together and serve.

CAULIFLOWER

If you have managed to grow just one perfect head of cauliflower, you may not know what to do with it. You can steam it and dress with melted butter, Hollandaise sauce, lemon butter, parslied bread crumbs, or a cheese sauce; or break it into flowerets and combine it with other more colorful vegetables. If you have managed to produce more than one of these lovely creamy heads, then you may need more culinary ideas.

A large part of my childhood was spent, it seemed, sitting at Sunday dinner, and one distinct memory is of a head of cauliflower nesting like a big fat hen in the middle of a round platter, surrounded by tiny ruby beets. I really didn't care for either one then, but the picture was pretty enough to persuade me to "try a little." A cauliflower has great possibilities for eye appeal and if its flavor seems too bland, it always can be enhanced by seasonings and sauces.

August

Cauliflower with Ham

    1 head cauliflower
    1 cup boiled ham, chopped
   ½ cup grated Parmesan cheese
  1½ cups sour cream
    2 tbsp. chopped chives
    1 tsp. Dijon mustard

Steam cauliflower in 1 inch of water in heavy saucepan until just tender, about 15-20 minutes. Test for doneness by inserting point of knife into heaviest part of stem. Drain well. Cut out core and break into flowerets. Butter a baking dish. Arrange one layer of cauliflower on bottom. Sprinkle over half of the ham and half of the cheese. Put in another layer of cauliflower and top with rest of ham and cheese. Stir mustard and chives into sour cream and pour over all. Bake at 350° about 20 minutes until heated through.

Cauliflower Polonaise

    1 head cauliflower
   ½ cup melted butter
   ¼ cup bread crumbs
    1 egg yolk, hard-boiled

Steam cauliflower in 1 inch of water in heavy pan. Stir crumbs into melted butter. Drain cauliflower and place in round serving dish. Pour over melted butter and crumbs. Sieve egg yolk over top.

August

CABBAGE

Here is another vegetable that changes its colors like a chameleon according to the way it is treated. Firstly, compare the tightly bound heads of pale white leaves you see in the winter with the loose-leaf fresh green cabbages of summer. Then think of the many ways in which you have been served this usually inglorious vegetable. No wonder it is unjustly scorned. But like Cinderella, it can be beautiful when given a chance.

The most badly treated cabbage I ever had was served in Ireland where I found they had defied all rules regarding vegetables. It had been allowed to grow to the size of a small bush and then was boiled and boiled and boiled. Heaven knows what the kitchen must have smelled like.

Usually I cook cabbage rapidly because we want it crisp, to mix with butter and sour cream or some caraway seeds or dill and bits of smoked ham or simply fried in butter with a good squeeze of lemon juice to add a lift in flavor.

Cabbage in Sour Cream

1 small cabbage, shredded
½ cup butter
1 egg
  salt and pepper
2 tbsp. sugar
1 cup sour cream
2 tbsp. lemon juice
1 tsp. caraway seeds

Sauté cabbage in butter until done but still crisp. Beat egg with sour cream and lemon juice. Mix with cabbage. Add sugar, salt and pepper and caraway seeds.

A stuffed cabbage contradicts the rule of rapid cooking because it needs a long slow simmer to produce an amalgamation of surprising flavors that are the mainstay of a cool night's meal. Cabbage braised in wine is a perfect accompaniment to a rolled pork or lamb shoulder or large veal sausages cooked in wine with a variety of mustards and pickles served alongside.

August

Stuffed Cabbage

1 head of cabbage
½ lb. sausage, cooked & crumbled
½ lb. chicken livers, cooked & diced
½ cup bread crumbs
1 egg
1 garlic clove, minced
2 tbsp. onion, minced
2 tbsp. chopped parsley
½ tsp. thyme
  salt, pepper, nutmeg
½ cup chicken stock
½ cup white wine
2 bacon slices

Blanch the cabbage in boiling, salted water for 5 minutes. Take it out and drain it. Dig out the core and spread the leaves apart. Make a dressing of sausage, livers, egg, seasonings and spread some on each leaf. When all stuffing has been used, tie up the cabbage to retain its shape. Place in a deep casserole. Cover with two slices bacon. Pour in ½ cup white wine and ½ cup chicken stock. Cover dish and bake in a 300° oven about 3 hours.

Cabbage Braised in Wine

1 head cabbage
4 tbsp. butter
1 tsp. salt
  freshly ground pepper
1 tsp. chopped fresh basil
½ cup dry white wine

Shred cabbage into fine strips. Melt butter in heavy frying pan. Add cabbage and toss until lightly browned. Add seasonings and wine. Cover and simmer until tender. Uncover and turn heat to high to evaporate moisture. Add more butter if necessary.

August

CUCUMBERS

Cukes by the bushel basket is the way we see them this time of year. Long green slims with unblemished, unwaxed skins, fresh and crunchy and ready for pickling if you're pickle minded (a few dills are fun to do), or wilted or creamed or made into boats filled with all kinds of delicious stuffings.

Cucumber soup is one of my main reasons for growing them at all—besides, it's another three meals a day item, spiced with dill and onion, lightly touched with cream. It goes down so easily that you'd better make a double batch. The only time I've ever been turned down on this favorite soup was by a guest who didn't like anything in that family: zucchini, melons, or cucumbers. Dinner that evening consisted of all of those things in one form or another, more's the pity. But all the more for the rest of us.

Cucumber Soup

2 large cucumbers
3 tbsp. butter
1 onion, chopped
1 tbsp. snipped dill
½ tsp. curry powder
1 quart chicken broth
1 cup light cream

Peel and seed cucumbers. Dice and add with chopped onion to butter in frying pan. Sauté 10 minutes. Add chicken broth, cover and simmer 15 minutes. Put in blender with dill and curry powder and salt and pepper. Blend until smooth. Chill. Before serving, add light cream and sprinkle chopped raw cucumber on top .

Cucumbers *can* be cooked, and are nice served with fish steaks—salmon, for instance.

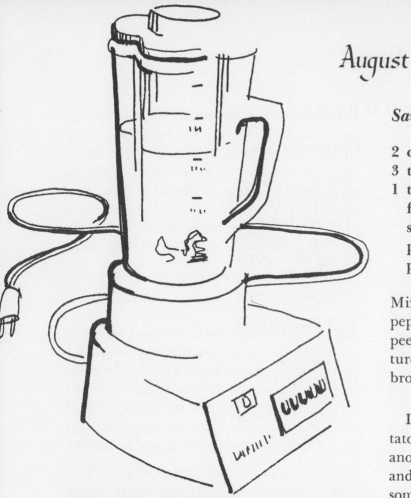

August

Sautéed Cucumbers

2 cucumbers
3 tbsp. butter
1 tbsp. oil
   flour
   salt
   pepper
   paprika

Mix together in small dish the flour, salt, pepper and paprika. Slice cucumbers, un-peeled, into ¼-inch slices. Dip in flour mixture and sauté in butter and oil until lightly browned on both sides.

Instead of celery, try cucumber in your potato, chicken, or shrimp salads. And for fish, another time make a sauce out of mayonnaise and sour cream with diced cucumber and some chopped dill or tarragon.

The indigestible cucumber can be tamed with the addition of sour cream or boiling in a sugar syrup. And when you think that you have a few too many, just make wilted cucumbers. They shrink.

If you have Hollandaise sauce for the salmon and a little runs over into the cucumbers, then inadvertently you have done a very nice thing.

Cucumbers in Sour Cream

2 cucumbers
1 tsp. salt
2 tsp. sugar
1 tsp. grated onion
2 tbsp. wine vinegar
2 tbsp. snipped dill
1 cup sour cream

Mix sour cream in bowl with vinegar, salt, sugar, onion, and dill. Taste to see if it is too sweet or too sharp. Slice unpeeled cucumbers and add to sauce. Let marinate a few hours before serving.

Stuffed Cucumbers

3 cucumbers
1 onion, minced
2 tomatoes, peeled and chopped
2 slices bacon, diced
1 tbsp. parsley
4 tbsp. bread crumbs
  salt and pepper

Peel cucumbers and cut in pieces 3 inches long. Scoop out centers. Fry bacon pieces until soft. Add onion and sauté until soft. Stir in tomatoes and cook until moisture is almost gone. Stir in parsley and bread crumbs. Season to taste. Fill cucumbers with mixture and place in baking dish. Pour in a little stock or water over bottom of dish. Bake at 350° until tender.

Ritz Cucumbers

1 cup water
½ cup sugar
⅓ cup vinegar
2 large cucumbers
  salad oil

Bring water, sugar, and vinegar to a full boil. Add cucumbers, peeled and thinly sliced. Stand over low heat for 2-3 minutes. Remove from stove and add 4 tbsp. oil. Cool. Let stand in refrigerator all day. Pour off extra liquid and serve.

Wilted Cucumbers

2 cucumbers
1 cup cold water
1 tbsp. salt
¼ cup French dressing
1 tsp. parsley, chopped

Peel cucumber and cut in paper-thin slices. Put in bowl and pour over water and salt. Let stand ½ hour. Drain and pat dry. Pour over French dressing and sprinkle with parsley.

EGGPLANT

Here we have the black beauty of the garden whose Anglo-Saxon name came from the smaller, rarer species that looks like a white hen's egg. Eggplant is called "aubergine" in France, and that name seems to suit this handsome specimen better.

It is too bad that so many people are put off by eggplant because it has not been prepared with imagination. Who could look at this vegetable and not be inspired to create something wonderful? It claims attention on its own when quickly sautéed or oven-fried, and it is a natural to combine with the other fruits of the garden at this time of year.

Parmesan cheese and herbs and tomatoes are a favorite grouping for a hot vegetable casserole. If you can catch some small ones—which you can because eggplant doesn't sneak up on you the way other vegetables do—they are perfect for stuffing individually.

Eggplant is one of those accommodating vegetables that can be served at any temperature. It reacts very kindly to being left overnight and eaten the next day as is, with just a crusty piece of bread for mopping up the juices.

August

Easy Eggplant

1 medium eggplant
 soft butter
1 cup bread crumbs
1 tbsp. chopped parsley
1 tbsp. chopped chives
1 tsp. chopped oregano
 salt and pepper

Cut unpeeled eggplant into slices ½ inch thick. Spread on both sides with soft butter. Mix herbs with bread crumbs, salt and pepper. Dip slices of eggplant into crumbs, covering both sides. Preheat oven to 450°. Place eggplant in one layer on baking sheet. Bake for 10 minutes. If browned and crisp, turn and bake on other side for 10 minutes until browned.

Eggplant Casserole

1 large eggplant, peeled and cubed
⅓ cup oil
½ cup diced celery
½ cup chopped onion
½ lb. macaroni shells, cooked
1 lb. ground lamb
1 clove garlic, minced
1 tsp. salt
½ tsp. pepper
1 tsp. chopped oregano
¼ tsp. ground cinnamon
1 cup chopped tomato
½ cup grated cheese

Sauté eggplant in oil. Remove. Sauté celery and onion. Add lamb and sauté until brown. Remove. Add garlic, tomatoes and herbs and seasonings and cook until most of moisture is evaporated. Put layer of eggplant in buttered casserole. Next a layer of celery-onion, then half of macaroni, then lamb, then tomato mixture. Repeat, ending with tomatoes. Sprinkle with grated cheese. Bake at 350° for 30 minutes.

If you like the old-world breads, the dark and chewy kinds, then you must make a crock of an extravagant-sounding dish called eggplant caviar, which can hang around your refrigerator getting better and better as the days go by. It keeps well because of the vinegar, oil, and lemon that go into it. What about a dinner that starts with eggplant caviar on black bread, goes on to cold cucumber soup, then broiled butterflied lamb leg, rice-stuffed tomatoes, and a honeydew melon with Port for dessert?

Eggplant Caviar

1 **good-sized eggplant**
2 **garlic cloves, crushed**
1 **small onion, chopped fine**
1 **tsp. salt**
1 **tsp. pepper**
1 **tbsp. capers, drained**
1 **tbsp. pine nuts**
¼ **tsp. ground cinnamon**

1 **tbsp. vinegar**
3 **tbsp. oil**
1 **tsp. lemon rind**
2 **tsp. lemon juice**
1 **tsp. chopped mint**

Bake the eggplant whole in a 350° oven for 45 minutes until soft. Peel and chop very fine. Add all other ingredients and mix well. Let stand several hours before using.

It really is not necessary to parboil eggplant, and no longer do we weight it under a flatiron to press out the excess water. There is a little trick in the cutting, though, to make the vegetable look a bit different from the last time you served it. When you make an eggplant Parmesan, slice it thinly the long way and use a round baking dish for the cooking. Then cut it in pie-shaped pieces for serving. I learned this in Italy where the eggplants actually grow in elongated shapes.

Eggplant Parmesan

1 large eggplant
2 eggs, beaten
  seasoned flour
  bread crumbs
  oil for frying
  grated Parmesan cheese
  tomato sauce

It is a little difficult to give exact amounts for this recipe, but you do want a lot more cheese than tomato sauce. Cut the unpeeled eggplant into very thin slices the long way. Dredge each slice with flour, dip in raw egg and then cover with crumbs. Heat oil in frying pan until hot. Quickly fry slices in oil until browned. Don't let eggplant absorb too much oil, which it would like to do. Work fast. When slices are all fried, place in oiled round casserole or pie plate. Layer with a lot of cheese and a little tomato sauce in between each layer. Top with 2 spoonfuls tomato sauce dribbled over and cheese sprinkled over all. Bake at 350° for 25 minutes until hot and cheese is melted and browned.

Stuffed Eggplants

Eggplants, small enough to serve one half per person. Cut in two lengthwise and score flesh with a sharp knife. Fry in oil, flesh side down until soft. Scoop out inside with spoon, chop, and mix with any of the following:
  1. cooked rice, green pepper, tomatoes, salt, pepper, oregano
  2. sautéed mushrooms, tomatoes, bread crumbs
  3. minced ham or bacon, grated cheese, minced onion, oregano, salt, pepper

Stuff and bake at 350° for 20 minutes.

August

ONIONS

Here is one of the oldest, most basic, most used flavors in our cooking. And how often do we think of onions until we are without? They stand straight and tall in the garden during the first half of the summer, adding a certain order to the rows. Then, as they near the time for use, they start to flag a bit and become raggedy until their tops are brown. It is almost time to pull them. I use my onions almost from the beginning, as scallions for a salad or to chop into the squash or blend into the soups. I hate not to use their lovely tops, but after a while, as they do get a bit tough and stringy, their best place is back in the garden for mulch.

Though onions make us shed oceans of tears, they reward us with their versatility. They can be stewed, stuffed, boiled, fried, baked, braised and added to almost every dish you can mention, with no adverse effects.

None, that is, if you like them. For the platter of stuffed vegetables that I suggested a while back, try a dressing of the onion itself, chopped with chicken livers, bacon, and some grated cheese.

Baked Onions

Put medium to large sized onions, unpeeled, into a baking dish. Roast in a 325° oven as you would a potato for 2 hours. Serve with salt, pepper, butter and a wisp of cinamon.

August

Stuffed Onions

- 4 large onions
- 2 strips bacon
- ½ lb. chicken livers
- ½ cup soft bread crumbs
- 1 tsp. salt
- ½ tsp. pepper
- ½ tsp. fresh chopped sage
- 2 tbsp. grated cheese

Peel onions without cuting off root end. Cut a slice from top of each. Boil onions and tops until just tender, about 30 minutes. Drain well. Remove centers. Fry bacon. Quickly sauté chicken livers in bacon fat. Chop livers and onion centers together very fine. Add salt, pepper, sage, chopped bacon, and crumbs. Stuff onions with mixture and sprinkle with cheese. Bake in a pan with a little liquid on the bottom. Bake at 375° for 20 minutes until tops are brown.

Onions braised in wine are a glossy accompaniment to chicken or beef, and one of my favorite recipes is a hand-me-down from a friend who always baked whole yellow onions in an amber sauce.

Glazed Onions

- 6 medium yellow onions
- 3 tbsp. butter
- 2 whole cloves
- salt
- pepper
- 1 cup dry red or white wine

Cut onions into ¼-inch slices; separate into rings. Heat butter in frying pan and add onions, stirring until well coated. Add cloves, salt and pepper and sauté until limp. Add wine, cover, and simmer 15 minutes until tender. Remove cover and cook until wine evaporates and onions are glazed.

Amber Onions

6 large yellow onions
1 tbsp. melted butter
1 tsp. salt
¼ tsp. paprika
2 tbsp. tomato juice
2 tbsp. honey

Peel onions, cut in halves crosswise. Place in buttered baking dish. Mix butter, tomato juice, honey, salt and paprika in pan and heat until honey melts. Pour over onions. Bake at 350°, covered, for 1 hour.

Did you know that onion peels are one of the world's oldest dyes and that the addition of these peelings to a pot of soup will help to give it a rich, dark hue? Grilled onions, halved or in thick slices, are lightly touched with oil and herbs to produce an unexpected second vegetable with roast meat. Perhaps the easiest yet most overlooked way to treat a medium to large sized onion is to bake it as you would a potato. Fancied up, for party fare, is the onion transformed into a tart, one of the nicest things that could happen to a vegetable so often taken for granted.

Onion Tart

1 recipe for pie crust fitted into a 10x15-inch jelly roll pan and pre-baked for 10 minutes at 425°.

8 medium onions
1 tsp. salt
½ tsp. chili powder
2 egg yolks
¼ cup butter
1 tsp. oil
3 tbsp. flour
½ cup light cream

Cut onions into thin slices. Sauté in butter and oil with salt and chili powder, covered, for 15 minutes. Remove cover and cook about 15 minutes more, until soft. Stir in flour. Add cream, beaten with yolks. Pour mixture into crust. Bake at 350° for 30 minutes. Broil just to get top browned. Cut into squares for serving.

August

POTATOES

Believe it or not, the potato has not been with us forever. As a matter of fact, it was so lacking in appearance that it was largely ignored by culinary artists until the 19th century, although the poor Irish had been busy exploring its possibilities for years. Finally, after a great deal of prodding, the chefs of Europe decided to see what they could do with the neglected tuber and, happily for us, they came forth with many delicious recipes.

Growing your own potatoes is the only way you can get tiny, marble-sized potatoes which should be dug, scrubbed, steamed in butter until tender, and sprinkled with fresh-cut herbs and served immediately. If you are calorie counting, then eat just potatoes, no meat or dessert. Greta Garbo kept her figure by never eating meat and potatoes together, always one or the other, and she preferred potatoes. When you dig your own, you may agree with her.

Is there anything better than a baked potato bursting open, with butter and salt and pepper, and steaming hot? Not for me the sour cream, chives, bacon, and all those other oddments. Just butter. I remember as a child having potatoes diced and cooked in heavy cream, the kind that was really heavy, and all the flavors melted into one glorious sort of potato stew—another once-a-year splurge.

Sena's Cream Potatoes

4 large potatoes
1 tsp. salt
½ tsp. pepper
1 cup heavy cream

Peel potatoes and cut into small dice. Soak in bowl of cold water for ½ hour. Drain and dry. Put into top of double boiler with cream and seasonings. Place over hot water and simmer for 1 hour until potatoes are tender and sauce is thick.

146

August

Potatoes don't wait well and they definitely do not reheat, so plan their cooking so they coincide with the serving of the meal—especially if you are serving an airy puff of potato and onion with your Sunday baked ham; or if you are doing escalloped potatoes baked in broth and layered with cheese in the Swiss manner. And if you are inordinately fond of garlic, there is a superb recipe using large amounts of it.

Potato Puff

4 large potatoes
½ cup melted butter
4 tbsp. minced onion
½-1 cup milk
1 tsp. salt
½ tsp. paprika
2 eggs, separated

Peel and boil potatoes until soft. Drain and return to heat. Shake pan until potatoes are dry. Put through ricer or food mill. Sauté onion in butter until soft but not browned. Beat egg yolks, salt, paprika, and butter-onion mixture into potatoes. Beat in enough milk to make a light, soft mixture. Beat whites until stiff. Fold into potatoes. Pour into buttered soufflé or baking dish. Bake at 350° for 45 minutes.

Savoyarde Potatoes

6 large potatoes
grated Swiss cheese
butter
1 tsp. salt
freshly ground pepper
¾ cup beef or chicken broth

Peel potatoes and cut into ⅛-inch thick slices. Butter well a casserole. Layer potatoes with grated cheese, dots of butter, and salt and pepper. Pour over the broth and sprinkle top with cheese. Bake at 325° for 1¼ hours until potatoes are tender and most of liquid has been absorbed.

August

Garlic Potatoes

3 lbs. potatoes
3 tbsp. butter
3 eggs
3 tbsp. flour
4 cloves garlic, crushed
3 tbsp. chopped parsley
½ tsp. nutmeg
1 tsp. salt
   freshly ground pepper

Peel potatoes. Boil until tender. Put through food mill or ricer. Beat in butter and eggs. Add flour, garlic, parsley and seasonings. Mix well. Put potatoes into shallow baking dish. Dot with butter. Bake at 350° for 15 minutes.

Potatoes with Sour Cream

4 medium potatoes
1 cup sour cream
2 eggs
2 tbsp. light cream or milk
2 tbsp. chopped chives
2 tbsp. chopped parsley
1 tsp. salt
   ground pepper
1 cup grated Cheddar or Swiss cheese

Cook potatoes in their skins until just tender. Cool slightly and peel and slice into rounds. Arrange slices in buttered shallow baking dish. Combine sour cream, eggs, milk, herbs, and seasonings. Pour over potatoes. Sprinkle with cheese. Bake at 350° for 30 minutes.

Sometimes the best cooks come a cropper on potato salad. I had a friend who really was an expert in the kitchen. Give her a complicated recipe and she could handle it without any trouble. I didn't know that her Achilles heel was potato salad, until she was asked to contribute a bowl of it to a community supper and called for help. The secret is to boil the potatoes whole with their skins on; then skin them and cut them up while hot and immediately marinate in French dressing. Throw in some chopped scallions at this time, then cool at room temperature all day. Before serving, dress with mayonnaise and sprinkle with fresh herbs.

Probably the worst insult that can be perpetrated on the poor potato is to French fry it the way most restaurants do. These potatoes, tasteless and sodden with grease, never suggest that the true French fried potato is a lovely golden tender stick, crisp on the outside and fluffy inside. They are definitely worth making at home—say, twice a year.

Potato chowder is a very satisfying meal in itself, and with other fresh vegetables added, it fills a need when your imagination and the larder are both a bit lacking.

Washington Chowder

    2 medium-sized potatoes
    1 small white onion
 1½ cups water
    1 cup chopped tomatoes
    2 tbsp. butter
    1 stalk celery
    1 cup corn kernels
    1 small green pepper
    1 tsp. salt
  ½ tsp. paprika
    2 cups milk

Peel potatoes and cut into small dice. Cook in water until tender. Sauté chopped onion, diced celery, and chopped green pepper in butter until soft. Add to potatoes. Add tomatoes and corn and cook until vegetables are done. Season to taste. Add milk and bring to a boil. Serve hot.

August

LIMA BEANS

Nature's ways really are very simple when you let her have her way. Her companion planting does go nicely from garden on to kitchen. The Indians knew this, and that is why we have that delectable combination of beans and corn called succotash. It has been refined a bit since Colonial days, when kidney beans were used instead of limas, with the addition of butter and cream. But it is still a simple marriage of flavors that cannot be improved upon.

I feel it worthwhile to grow my own limas just for this. Actually, it isn't the growing; it's the shelling that takes time and patience —although it may be well into August before you see the full pods hanging on the bean bushes. Don't pick them until they are firm and fat. More reluctant to open than pea pods, limas take a knife and a strong thumb to split and, of course, there aren't as many inside. But cooked until just tender and dressed with heavy cream and an abundance of chopped chives, or covered with a lemony sauce, they are well worth the effort involved.

Limas with Cream and Bacon

3 lbs. lima beans in pods
3 strips bacon
1 cup heavy cream
2 tbsp. chopped chives

Shell limas and cook in boiling salted water until tender. Cook bacon and chop. Mix chives with cream. Pour off all but two tbsp. of bacon fat. Toss limas briskly in fat. Pour in cream and heat through. Sprinkle with bacon and serve.

Lima Beans Poulette

3 lbs. limas in pods
2 tbsp. flour

3 tbsp. butter
1 cup chicken stock
  juice of 1 lemon
2 tbsp. cream
1 egg yolk
1 tbsp. chopped parsley

Shell beans and cook in salted water until tender. Drain. Melt butter in saucepan, stir in flour and cook for 2 minutes, stirring. Stir in stock and lemon juice and cook until it boils. Take off heat and quickly blend in egg yolk beaten with cream. Add parsley, season to taste and pour over beans. Reheat without boiling.

Someone passed this recipe along to me with the words, "It sounds dreadful, but you must try it." It did sound strange, but I was pleasantly surprised. On first thought, sour cream, maple syrup, and Tabasco didn't seem a very palatable combination for anything, much less garden-fresh limas. But we had a good crop and I experimented.

Maple Limas

3 lbs. limas in pods
1 cup sour cream
2 tbsp. dry mustard
2 tbsp. maple syrup
  dash of Tabasco sauce

Pod limas and cook in boiling salted water until just tender. Heat sour cream with maple syrup, dry mustard, and Tabasco stirred in. Fold limas into sauce and serve hot.

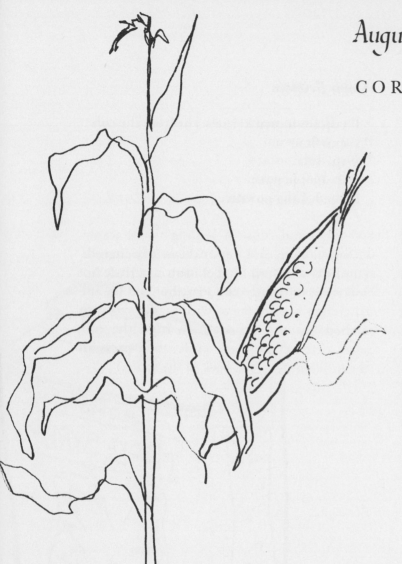

August

CORN

I'm not saving the best until last, although August is rapidly running out on us and somehow corn seems to bring summer and early autumn together. Perhaps it is because the corn starts out young and sweet and tiny, just right for eating off the cob, and it grows with the summer, getting more golden and a little chewier until we start to use it for puddings and chowders and finally for relish. Then we must honestly face the fact that summer is stretching into the golden haze of autumn. Corn bridges nicely the gap between the seasons, blunting the shock of change and making us less rueful for the passing of another summer, as its leaves turn from green to gold to brown and the stalks turn into shocks.

Corn is surely as American as the proverbial apple pie, which we'll get to later, and no American should be caught overcooking its

August

tender kernels. Straight from picking to pot is the rule. If you must hold it for a while before cooking, immediately put it unhusked in the refrigerator.

The first corn of the season is eaten with reverence. Husked, boiled for no more than 6 minutes, brushed with butter and salted, it is eaten from the cob with plenty of napkins handy. Except for the toothless, either young or old, corn on the cob is the all-American favorite during August. We try to eat our fill.

And when we have, think about the dozens of other ways to serve this wondrous vegetable. It combines with almost everything else that is in the garden (or the henyard), making up into creamy puddings and soufflés, spicy casseroles, crisp fritters to soak in syrup, smooth timbales, and hearty breads to serve with hot chilis on cool fall nights.

Corn Fritters

1 cup fresh corn kernels, cut from the cob
¼ cup flour
½ tsp. salt
   dash of pepper
1 tsp. baking powder
1 egg

Combine corn and egg. Add to dry ingredients in bowl. Drop by spoonfuls in a little hot bacon fat in frying pan. Fry, flip, and fry until golden brown. Serve with maple syrup or melted butter. (To cut corn from the cob, score with a very sharp knife, then press all the milk out with the back of the knife.)

August

Corn Timbales

1 cup raw scraped corn
4 eggs
1 tsp. grated onion
1 tsp. salt
1 cup heavy cream
  dash of Tabasco

Combine corn with eggs, salt, onion, and Tabasco. Whip cream and fold into corn mixture. Butter well individual custard cups. Fill ⅔ full and place on a rack or several thicknesses of paper in a pan of hot water. Bake at 325° for 20-30 minutes, until set. Turn out and serve with a mushroom sauce made by whirling ¼ lb. mushrooms, ½ cup sour cream, ½ cup consommé, 2 tbsp. flour, 2 tbsp. butter, and salt and pepper in a blender until smooth. Heat until thick.

Corn Bread

⅓ cup sugar
¼ cup bacon fat
4 slices bacon
1 egg
1 tsp. salt
1 cup milk
1 cup yellow cornmeal
1 cup flour
3 tsp. baking powder
½ cup corn kernels, raw or cooked

Put flour, cornmeal, sugar, baking powder and salt in bowl. Fry bacon until crisp. Crumble. Stir egg, milk, bacon fat into dry ingredients. Add bacon bits and corn. Mix quickly. Pour into well-buttered 9-inch square pan. Bake at 400° for 30 minutes.

A dish we start talking about when the first ears of corn appear is a baked corn pudding, an old recipe that comes down from somebody's great-grandmother and must be made with the late, chewy, yellow kernels. Another pudding that resembles a soufflé can be made with any corn, early, middle, or late. Throughout the season we cook the corn in cream or sauté it in bacon fat with the addition of green pepper and onion.

Baked Corn

24 ears fresh corn
 2 tsp. salt
    freshly ground pepper
 1 tbsp. sugar
½ lb. butter

With a sharp knife, score each row of corn kernels. With back of knife press out all pulp into bowl. Mix in salt, pepper, sugar and butter cut into small pieces. Pour into greased baking dish. Bake uncovered at 375° for about 45 minutes until top is a crusty golden brown.

Corn Pudding

 2 cups fresh corn kernels
 2 eggs
1½ cups milk
 2 tbsp. flour
 1 tbsp. melted butter
 1 tbsp. sugar
    salt and pepper

Beat eggs; add corn and milk. Mix flour and butter together and beat in. Season with sugar, salt, and pepper. Pour into buttered baking dish. Bake at 375° uncovered for 45 minutes or until firm.

August

Corn in Cream

8 ears fresh corn
1 cup heavy cream
1 tbsp. sugar

Cut kernels off cobs. Put into top of double boiler with cream and sugar. Cook over boiling water 40 minutes or until corn is tender. Before serving, season to taste with salt. For succotash, add cooked lima beans, butter and pepper.

Corn and chicken chowder is not only alliterative but is pleasing to the taste buds. Corn casseroles are numberless in the world of corn cuisine but always are a beautiful sight on a buffet table.

Corn and Chicken Chowder

2 cups fresh corn kernels
2 cups cooked chicken, cubed
2 medium-sized onions
2 medium-sized potatoes
2 slices salt pork or bacon
2 cups chicken broth
1 quart milk
  salt and pepper

Peel potatoes and cut into small dice. Parboil for 5 minutes. Cut salt pork or bacon into small dice and sauté in skillet until crispy. Remove from frying pan. Add onions to fat and sauté until translucent. Add corn, potatoes, and onions to chicken broth and simmer until vegetables are done. Add chicken pieces and milk. Bring to a boil and season to taste with salt and pepper.

August

Colache

3 zucchinis
2 tbsp. butter
2 tbsp. bacon fat or oil
1 large onion
4 ears fresh corn
2 green peppers, seeded
4 peeled tomatoes
   salt and pepper
   Tabasco sauce

Cut unpeeled zucchini into rounds and sauté in butter and fat until slightly browned. Slice onion and green peppers and add to pan. Sauté briefly. Add cut-up tomatoes. Cut corn from cob and stir in. Season with salt, a lot of freshly ground pepper, and 2 drops Tabasco. Cover and cook for ½ hour. Uncover and cook for 15 minutes.

Before we leave this engrossing subject, I must impart one bit of knowledge which may be of interest to those who have trouble digesting corn. Try scoring the kernels with the point of a knife before eating it off the cob. In this way you will get only the soft inside of the kernel, not the rough outer skin.

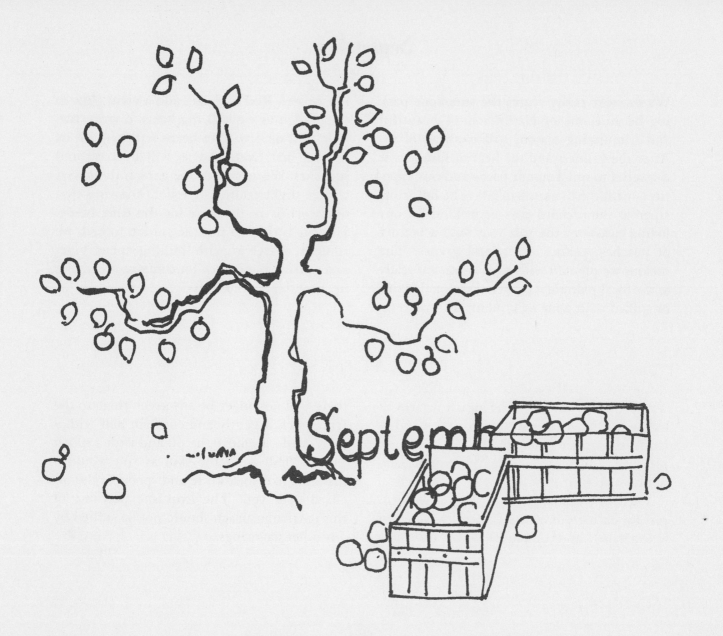

September

WE CANNOT really regret the summer's passing because one of Nature's most beautiful and stimulating seasons still is ahead of us. After the fullness and the heat of summer, it is a relief to quicken our pace—and our appetites—with the briskness of fall. The fall fruits ripen as the orchard pays us in kind for our loving care over the past year with a bounty of peaches, pears, apples, and grapes. The melons we planted with high hopes are ready as the focal point of a platter of seasonal fruits, or spiked with wine or liqueur, for a refreshing dessert. Red cabbages add a vivid glow to the garden as we still dig beets, carrots, turnips, and onions. The beans will be with us until a first frost, and so will broccoli and squashes. We approach the garden these days with a slight feeling of relief, knowing that our work is really done for the time being. Until it is time to put the garden to bed, we content ourselves with pulling spent vines and putting them back for compost or tidying up, as the spirit moves us.

PEACHES

Truly the nectar fruit, the peach arrives at the propitious moment when most other fruits of summer have gone by; and the pure pleasure of biting into a fragrant sample cannot be surpassed.

The white peach, Belle of Georgia, we grow just for eating out of hand, literally. When it is dead ripe—and you can tell this by the color: there will no longer be any green tinge to the fruit—pick it gently and cut it in half with a sharp knife. Remove the pit and with a spoon eat the flesh from the skin as you would a melon. Take your knife and spoon to the orchard with you. The exquisite perfume of this particular peach should not be sullied by any other flavorings.

The other types of peaches, the golden ones, can be sliced or halved and rolled in a combination of half honey, half brandy, and left to chill until serving time. They can be baked in wine or poached in a simple sugar syrup, marinated in orange juice or made into a rich custard tart.

Wine-Baked Peaches

4 ripe peaches
4 macaroons
   apricot or peach brandy
¼ cup dry white wine

Dip peaches in boiling water for a count of ten to loosen skins. Peel, cut in half and remove pits. Crumble macaroons and soak in sufficient brandy to moisten. Place peach halves in flat baking dish and pour in wine. Fill halves with macaroons. Bake at 350° for 20 minutes. Serve hot, with custard sauce, if desired.

Poached Peaches

4 ripe peaches
1½ cups water
1 cup sugar
2 tbsp. orange liqueur (optional)

Cook sugar and water in deep saucepan until sugar is dissolved. Peel peaches and add to syrup. Simmer whole until fruit is tender. Remove fruit to bowl. Boil syrup until it is thick. Add liqueur if desired. Pour over fruit and chill.

September

Open Peach Pie

Pastry: 1½ sticks butter
  1½ cups flour
   4 tbsp. powdered sugar
   ½ tsp. ground nutmeg

Combine ingredients in bowl and mix with fingers until a sticky dough is formed. Press into 9-inch pie or tart pan. Prick with fork. Refrigerate for 15 minutes. Bake at 425° for 10 minutes. Cool.

Filling: 5 medium-sized peaches
   ¾ cup sugar
   ½ tsp. cinnamon
   3 egg yolks
   ⅔ cup heavy cream
   ⅓ cup brown sugar

Fill pie shell with sliced peaches. Sprinkle ¾ cup sugar and cinnamon over peaches. Bake at 400° for 15 minutes. Pour egg yolks and cream beaten together over fruit. Sprinkle brown sugar over all. Bake at 350° until filling is set, another 20-30 minutes.

A buttered pound cake layered with peaches that have been stewed in a rum and ginger syrup is a magnificent dessert for a party. Or a modified version of rich Southern Syllabub will make everyone leave the table in a happy frame of mind.

September

Frozen Peach Pudding

1 pound cake in a loaf shape
4 cups peach slices
1/3 cup water
1 cup sugar
1/4 cup dark rum
1/2 tsp. ground ginger

Slice pound cake the long way into five layers. It is easier to slice neatly when it is still frozen. Scrape off the dark brown crust on the top layer. Combine water, sugar, rum, and ginger in saucepan and boil until sugar dissolves. Add sliced peaches and cook until soft. Drain peaches and return syrup to pan. Boil until it reduces to about 1 cup. Place sliced peaches on layers of cake, omitting top layer. Pour syrup over, soaking well. Place in freezer for at least 24 hours. Serve with whipped cream.

Peach Syllabub

2 cups sliced peaches
1/2 cup powdered sugar
1 cup heavy cream
2 egg whites
2 tbsp. Cream Sherry

Add 1/4 cup powdered sugar to cream; whip until stiff. Beat egg whites stiff with remaining sugar. Combine and blend two mixtures. Add wine. Pour over fruit.

Peaches also can be used as a color note with main course dishes if they are broiled or baked, or incorporated into the sauce for Cornish hens, for instance. They like spices such as ginger or cinnamon or flavorings of almond or rum and their sweetness contrasts well with the sharp tang of a chutney or ginger marmalade.

September

Cornish Hens in Peach Sauce

4 Cornish game hens
1 lemon
2 tbsp. oil
1 tbsp. butter
  salt and pepper
1 cup chicken broth
½ cup Port wine
¼ cup chutney
2 peaches
2 tbsp. butter

Thaw game hens and wipe dry. Sprinkle insides with salt and pepper and place a quarter of lemon in each. Brown in oil and butter on all sides. Place in deep casserole. Season. Blend the broth, wine and chutney until smooth. Pour over game hens. Cover and bake at 350° for 45 minutes. Peel and slice peaches and sauté briefly in butter. Remove cover of baking dish and add peach slices. Bake for 15 minutes.

Like all fruits, peaches should be served at room temperature. Their flavor dissipates when they are cold.

PLUMS

I remember being terribly disillusioned when I first learned that all things were not as I thought they should be. It was when I discovered one Christmas that plum pudding is not made with plums—with currants and raisins, yes, but not plums as I thought of them. I now know that raisins are not grapes but dried up plums in England, but I'll never be quite sure just what Jack Horner pulled out of that pie.

Our plums are large and juicy and come in many colors and with many names. They can be made into wine, catsup, vinegar, jam, butter, a sinfully rich plum cake and a nice old-fashioned dessert reminiscent of floating island called Plum Trifle. Or they can be eaten when they are ripe and full of juice as they come off the tree. I suppose they can also be dried into prunes.

Plum Cake

½ lb. butter
2 cups sugar
4 eggs
2 cups flour
1 tsp. salt
2 tsp. baking powder
1 tsp. vanilla
about 18 plums
1 tsp. cinnamon
extra sugar, butter

Cream together the butter and sugar until light. Add eggs, beating well. Stir in flour, baking powder and salt mixed together. Add vanilla. Spread batter in buttered 8x12-inch pan. Halve plums and place pitted on batter close together. Sprinkle 1 tsp. cinnamon mixed with 2 tbsp. sugar over top. Pour 3 tbsp. melted butter over all. Bake at 325° for 1 hour until done.

Sauce:
½ lb. plums halved and pitted
2 cinnamon sticks
2 lemon slices
1½ cups water
sugar to taste
1 tbsp. butter
1 tbsp. arrowroot flour mixed
with 4 tbsp. cold water

Add cinnamon sticks, lemon, and sugar to water. Boil until sugar dissolves. Add plums and cook until mushy. Stir in arrowroot and cook until clear and thick. Add butter. Serve hot over cake.

September

Plum Trifle

1 lb. plums
3 egg whites
2 tbsp. sugar
1 recipe boiled custard
   milk

Cook plums slowly until soft in a little water. Mash or blend and let cool. To each cup of pulp add three egg whites beaten stiff with 2 tbsp. sugar. Drop spoonfuls of this on half-inch simmering milk in a flat pan. Poach for 2 minutes on one side; turn and poach for 2 minutes. Drain on paper towels. Drop onto custard and serve.

MELONS

A description given to melons as having a "musky spiciness" may be because of a type known as the nutmeg melon. It is a member of the cantaloupe group and they are all members of the gourd family, which takes in pumpkins, squash, and cucumbers. Having firmly established the family background of this interesting fruit, we can go on to its many uses.

One naturally visualizes melons as part of a compote of fruits, or served in wedges with lime or lemon quarters, or fashioned into balls and sprinkled with chopped candied ginger, fresh mint, or a little liqueur of some kind. A splurge that I used to be very fond of was half a cantaloupe or Crenshaw filled with vanilla ice cream, which I ate while my grandfather carefully sprinkled his half with salt and pepper. Today I forego the ice cream and use the salt—no pepper.

Curried melon is a spicy relish for plain meatloaf or chicken, and an underripe melon may be sautéed in egg and crumbs or scalloped for a vegetable.

September

Curried Melon

1 underripe melon
  butter
1 onion, minced
1 tbsp. butter
1 tsp. curry powder

Peel and cut melon into cubes or 1-inch thick slices. Fry in a little butter. In another pan fry the onion until golden. Add curry powder and cook 5 minutes. Add melon. Cover and cook until tender, adding a little water if necessary.

A dead-ripe cantaloupe or Crenshaw is perfect for a surprising melon tart. A frozen melon roll flavored with wine and spices makes a different and glamorous early fall dessert.

Melon Tart

2 cups of melon cubes
½ lb. sugar
1 cup water
1 baked 8-inch pie shell
2 egg whites
2 tbsp. sugar

Make a syrup of sugar and water. Add melon cubes and simmer 5-6 minutes until soft. Remove melon and reduce syrup by boiling until thick. Add desired flavoring. Place melon cubes in pie shell and pour syrup over them. Whip egg whites into a meringue with sugar and spread over pie. Brown for 15 minutes in a 350° oven.

September

Melon Roll

1 pint heavy cream
1 tsp. gelatin
½ cup sugar
1 cup melon pulp, drained
   chopped melon pieces
   chopped candied ginger
   white wine

Whip until stiff the cream with ½ cup sugar. Fold in drained melon pulp and softened gelatin. Line a melon mold with this and freeze. When frozen fill center with chopped melon mixed with ginger and white wine to taste. Cover tightly and freeze for several hours. Unmold and slice across into circles.

To me, the delicate pale green honeydews are best when sliced into crescents and wrapped with thin slices of prosciutto ham. Very often this is served as a first course, but one could make it a whole meal with a crusty bread stick or two. Just for fun, "plug" a melon someday. It is not hard to do and makes a good talking point when the dessert course comes around. And if you like to use the melon ball gadget, make a whole bowlful and then douse them with sugar and rum and candied ginger.

Plugged Melon

Cut a deep plug about 2 inches square in a ripe melon. Remove plug and score inside of flesh with ice pick. Slowly pour in light rum, Port or cognac, as much as the melon will take. Replace plug and seal it closed. Refrigerate for 24 hours, turning melon occasionally.

September

APPLES

Although we do import some from as far away as South Africa, it seems that the apple is ours alone. For apples are the number one American fruit, and we have them early, mid-season, and late, right on through the winter. Especially they are a piece of fall. Their crisp, juicy tang tastes as though they breathed the winey air of autumn, capturing its very essence. And we savor this as we serve them with cheese, in pies, baked, fried, stewed, poached, in sauces, soups and slumps. It's a marvelously versatile fruit, and according to health experts, is so very, very good for us as well.

Like the tomatoes and corn, apples appear in every culinary form, and there are so many ways of using them that their niche in the recipe file is stuffed. They get along with almost every other member of the fruit and vegetable kingdom and enhance the flavor of meat and poultry, too.

The apple season in my orchard means the anticipated sugary crisps, spicy pies, special meat loaves, turnovers, puddings, and every morning for breakfast baked apples stuffed with a variety of dried fruits and spices and sweetened with maple syrup or honey.

September

Apple Gingerbread

2 tbsp. butter
2 eggs
½ cup sour cream
½ cup molasses
½ cup brown sugar
1½ cups flour
1 tsp. baking soda
2 tsp. ginger
1 tsp. cinnamon
½ tsp. salt
½ cup melted butter
2 apples

In 9-inch square pan melt 2 tbsp. butter. Pare, core, and slice apples and arrange in pan. Sprinkle with 3 tbsp. brown sugar and 1 tsp. cinnamon. Beat eggs; add sour cream, molasses, and rest of brown sugar. Mix the other dry ingredients and add to eggs, blending well. Stir in melted butter. Pour batter over apples. Bake at 350° for 30 minutes until cake tests done. Serve with whipped cream or vanilla ice cream.

Special Apple Pie

Pie crust for a 2-crust 9-inch pie
2 pared diced fresh pears
2 tbsp. rum
4 or 5 diced, pared tart apples
¼ cup ground almonds, toasted
¾ to 1 cup sugar
2 tbsp. flour
½ tsp. cinnamon
2 tbsp. butter

Line 9-inch pie pan with pastry. Sprinkle almonds over bottom. Put in pears and sprinkle with rum. Toss apples with sugar, flour and cinnamon. Heap over pears. Dot with butter. Put on top crust. Seal edges and prick top with fork. Bake at 450° for 10 minutes. Turn heat to 350° and bake 45 minutes.

September

Rolled Apple Meat Loaf

1 lb. ground chuck
½ lb. ground pork
½ lb. ground veal
1 tbsp. Worcestershire
1 tbsp. chopped parsley
½ tsp. ground nutmeg
1 minced onion
  salt and pepper
2 eggs
2 slices bread, crusts off
¼ cup orange juice
3 cooking apples

Heat orange juice and soak bread slices in it. Mix together meats, Worcestershire, eggs, bread and orange juice, salt and pepper. Roll out meat mixture on waxed paper into a rectangle ½ inch thick. Pare, core, and dice apples. Sprinkle parsley, onion, apples and nutmeg over meat. Roll up, jellyroll fashion, and place on buttered baking sheet. Bake at 350° for 1 hour. Remove to serving platter and garnish with sautéed apple slices and parsley.

Apple Turnovers

1 recipe short pie pastry
6 cups apples, peeled, cored, and sliced
½ cup apricot jam
2 tbsp. cognac
1 tsp. grated lemon rind
1 tbsp. butter
½ tsp. nutmeg
  sugar to taste
1 egg beaten with a little water

Put apples in saucepan with jam, cognac, nutmeg, rind, butter. Stew til very soft. Mash and add sugar to taste. Cook down until very thick. Roll out pastry and cut into 5-inch circles. Put a spoonful of apple mixture on one half of circle. Fold other half over to make a half moon and press edges together with tines of fork. Brush with egg. Bake at 400° for 15 minutes until golden. Serve warm.

September

Baked Apples

4 firm apples
  raisins
  butter
  sugar
  cinnamon
  cider

Core apples and pare 1 inch down from top. Cream together some butter, cinnamon and sugar. Put a bit in each apple. Put in a few raisins. Fill with butter. Place in baking dish and pour cider in to cover bottom. Bake at 350° for 45 minutes, basting occasionally.

In the Normandy section of France, which is famous for its apple dishes and for Calvados, its apple brandy, they blend their apples with cream and the brandy to create a mellow rich sauce.

Chicken Normandy

1 fryer, cut up
3 late fall apples, peeled and chopped
2 oz. apple brandy
½ cup heavy cream
  salt and pepper
6 tsp. butter

Brown chicken until golden in butter. Remove and add more butter and apples to pan. Sauté apples. Put apples on bottom of baking dish. Put chicken pieces on top. Pour over remaining butter and sprinkle with a little salt and pepper. Cover and cook for 20 minutes. Pour in brandy and cream. Cook for 15 minutes. Uncover and let sauce thicken for 10 minutes.

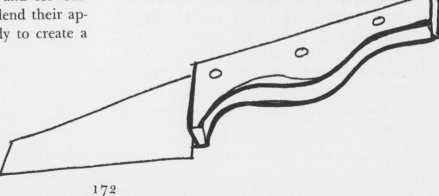

September

One of the most useful qualities of an apple is its high liquid content when added to meat loaves, breads and muffins. The English, who are exceedingly fond of pies, and not just for dessert, combine apples with pork to make a good main dish pie which is eaten either hot or cold.

Polished apples in a wooden bowl, with walnuts or chestnuts, and served with a tray of assorted cheeses, make the perfect ending to a rich meal—perfect also because apples are said to have super-digestive powers.

PEARS

My favorite in the springtime because of its lovely blossoms, the pear tree is also the easiest to keep up, as it requires no pruning. Pears should not be left to fully ripen on the tree. Pick them when they are quite yellow and bring them in to finish ripening at room temperature. Then try them with cheese come to room temperature, also, and a bottle of white wine.

We so enjoy the Bartletts' slightly musky flavor that we plan to eat them plain. If you have an overabundance, however, there is no reason why you can't poach them in red wine or bake them in a sugar syrup or orange juice with a sprinkling of ground ginger and toasted almonds.

September

Pears in Red Wine

4 early pears
1½ cups Claret
⅓ cup sugar
1 piece cinnamon stick
8 whole cloves
2 tbsp. brandy

Put Claret, sugar, and cinnamon into sauce-pan and cook until sugar dissolves. Peel pears and leave whole. Put two cloves into flower end of each pear. Place pears in wine syrup and simmer until tender, about 20 minutes. Turn occasionally so they color evenly. Remove pears to serving bowl and reduce sauce to half by boiling hard. Add 2 tbsp. brandy and pour over fruit. Chill.

The later, hard pears (Bosc or Seckle) definitely are for cooking. Try stuffing the cavities with dried fruit and baking them. Or poach them in plain sugar and water and serve with a rum custard or hard sauce; or make into a soft creamy pudding flavored with almond and nutmeg.

Winter pears bake beautifully and hold their shape better than their summer sisters, the Bartletts. They also affiliate themselves very well with spices and liqueurs, absorbing other flavors and scents and giving a welcome fillip to a hearty dinner.

Pear Pudding

3 large winter pears
2 tbsp. butter
½ tsp. nutmeg
3 eggs
½ cup brown sugar
2 cups milk
½ tsp. almond extract

Peel, core, and slice pears. Melt butter and coat pears. Sprinkle nutmeg over fruit and cover. Cook until tender but not mushy. Place pears in baking dish. Beat egg, sugar, milk and almond extract together. Pour over pears. Place in pan filled with hot water. Bake at 325° for 45 minutes until set. Chill.

September

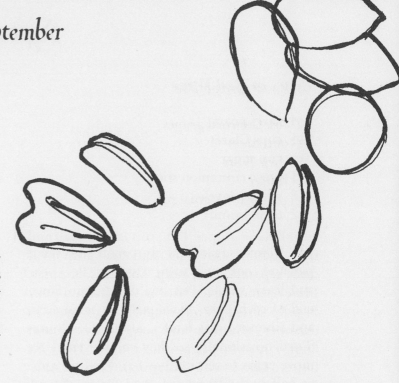

Fruit-Filled Pears

⅓ cup chopped walnuts
½ cup chopped mixed dried fruits
   butter
   brown sugar
 3 large ripe Bosc pears
¼ cup white wine

Cut pears in half and remove cores. Mix together the nuts and fruit. Pack into centers of pears. Put pears close together in shallow buttered baking dish. Pour in wine. Bake, uncovered, at 350° for 30-40 minutes, until pears are tender.

GRAPES

The grapes hanging high in elegant clusters may outfox the fox of fable fame but they do not seem to fool the birds who find them as tasty as we do, and we hope there are enough for all. The time is at hand, however, for our once-a-year pie made from the glorious purple Concords and to make jars and jars of pure grape jelly, using partially-underripe fruit for added flavor and pectin. When the grapes are at their ripest, I make juice, using a mixture of the various kinds in the arbor.

September

Concord Grape Pie

2 lbs. Concord grapes
¾ cup sugar
1½ tbsp. flour
  butter
  pastry for 2-crust pie

Slip skins off grapes. Put pulp in saucepan and skins in bowl. Cover pan and cook pulp until seeds separate from pulp, about 10 minutes. Place colander over bowl with skins and pour in pulp. Press pulp through, leaving seeds in colander. Mix skins and pulp with sugar and flour. Pour into pastry-lined pie pan. Dot with butter. Cover with pastry top. Bake at 450° for 10 minutes. Reduce heat to 350° and bake for 30 minutes longer.

Snow grapes are fun to make and to use just for decorating a cake or cookie platter. Grapes also can be incorporated successfully into any kind of fruit compote. Be sure to split and seed them. And while you are seeding, do some for a special grape tart that al-ways causes a gasp of admiration when presented at the dining table. It is a dessert that captures the feeling of the fall harvest perfectly with a lovely mosaic of different colored grapes glazed with a deep ruby jelly.

Snow Grapes

Wash and dry clusters of grapes. Partially beat an egg white in a bowl. Dip the grapes in the egg white and then in sifted powdered sugar until they are covered. Let dry.

Mosaic Tart

  Use tart pastry
1-2 cups red, green, and purple or
    black grapes, halved
  1 cream cheese (8 oz.)
  3 tbsp. frozen orange juice concentrate
½ cup currant jelly
  2 tbsp. Kirsch

Make pastry and press into tart pan. Bake for 15 minutes at 425°. Cool. Beat softened cream cheese with orange juice until soft and spreadable. Spread in tart shell. Halve and seed grapes and make a pattern on cream cheese, putting grapes very close together. You can alternate colors or circles of colors. Make a glaze by melting jelly with Kirsch. Paint whole top with glaze covering all spaces, especially in between fruit. Keep refrigerated until ½ hour before serving.

RED CABBAGE

When I see red cabbages growing, I am always reminded of a fall trip I once made with a friend who was in the business of making flower arrangements. We passed a field of red cabbages that had gone by and were leafing out in all directions. She insisted that we stop because they would be perfect sprayed with gold for Christmas decorations. It took her professional eye to see it, while I was just bemoaning that they were too old to use for a wonderful recipe we like to make when there's some game in the larder. It is just as good, too, with goose or a pork roast with its rich combination of wine, currant jelly, spices and

chestnuts. This means, I guess, that red cabbage has its place either on the mantelpiece or in the braising pan.

Red Cabbage

1 head red cabbage
2 onions, chopped
3 tbsp. bacon fat
6 oz. red wine
6 oz. currant jelly
1 tart apple, chopped

4 tbsp. brown sugar
6 whole cloves
10 whole chestnuts, peeled
½ cup red wine vinegar

Slice cabbage thin. Melt bacon fat and sauté onions. Add cabbage, red wine, jelly, and wine vinegar. Cover and simmer 1 hour, watching to see that it does not burn. Add water if necessary. Add apple, brown sugar, cloves, and chestnuts. Simmer until cabbage and nuts are tender, about 40 minutes.

TURNIPS

Another of the root cellar vegetables that suffered for many years from lack of loving preparation is the turnip. It deserves a better fate than to be mashed and mixed with potatoes or dumped ignominiously on a plate just at Thanksgiving.

To begin at the turnip's beginning, try serving it raw for an hors d'oeuvre with the other crisp garden edibles. Then braise or mash with some interesting seasonings. Don't play the turnip down; build it up with the addition of sour cream and basil or savory.

Bake the rutabagas whole for about an hour or a little more in a 375° oven and serve

September

them right in their skins with lots of butter, salt and pepper. Try turnip in custard for a complete change of pace; it has a lovely, light soufflé-like texture. Turnips may take a little more imagination than beans or broccoli but they are with us longer, and there's more time to experiment.

Braised Turnips

1 lb. yellow turnips
2 tbsp. butter
  sugar
¾ cup beef broth
1 tbsp. lemon juice

Peel turnips. Slice them thickly. Melt butter and cook turnips slowly in frying pan. When they have softened a bit, add meat stock and sprinkle some sugar over all. Simmer until tender, uncover and let glaze. Sprinkle with lemon juice before serving.

Turnip Puree

Peel turnips and cook in boiling salted water until very soft. Mash very fine. Put back in pan and beat in sugar, sour cream, and a pinch of basil.

Turnips in Custard

1 large yellow turnip
2 eggs
1 cup cream
  salt and pepper
  sugar
  nutmeg

Peel turnip and boil it until soft enough to mash well. Beat eggs and cream together. Add seasonings. Mix with turnip. Place in buttered baking dish set in pan of hot water. Bake at 350° for 30 minutes until set.

ctober

October

THE GEESE wake us at dawn each morning as they fly high overhead toward their winter home, their loud cries warning that autumn is here.

The first frost has left its mark on the garden and the stark, blackened vines bear a few tomatoes, some squashes, and a cucumber or two that did not make the final harvest. We gardeners are rather glad it is over, for there is time enough for all things, and now it's time for the growing season to end.

We must collect ourselves and our thoughts now, as we must tidy the garden and prepare it for the winter. The pumpkins are picked and piled up to look festive for Hallowe'en. We'll make jack o'lanterns from the biggest and use the smaller, sweeter pie pumpkins for eating. The leaves on the fruit trees are turning golden as we add late pears and apples to our harvest.

The gardener knows the seasons better than other people, for he tells time by Nature's world, by what the garden yields each week or month. It has given us a purposeful feeling to complete the cycle, to know the beginning and the end. Now with some feeling

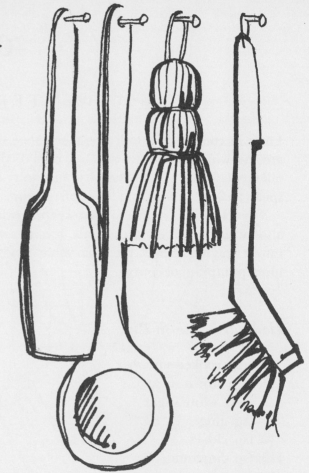

of relief we put away the gardening tools, but deep down we know that in a few months we'll welcome getting them out again. It is this eternal continuity that makes a gardener's life one of hope and optimism.

October

WINTER SQUASHES

Long in coming but welcome when they do are the winter squashes, much a part of the fall scene. Their golden flesh has an affinity to spices and to the nuts and fruits of autumn.

The Hubbard is the longest keeping and also by far the largest of them all. It makes up into a fragrant, spicy pie, somewhat resembling pumpkin, of course.

Hubbard Squash Pie

    2 cups cooked squash
    ⅔ cup brown sugar
    4 tbsp. white sugar
    ½ tsp. ginger
    ¼ tsp. cloves
    1½ tsp. cinnamon
    ½ tsp. nutmeg
    1½ cups milk
    2 eggs
    1 9-inch pie shell, prebaked for
      10 minutes at 425°

Steam a piece of squash until soft and purée in blender. Drain liquid off. Mix squash with sugar and spices. Beat in eggs and milk. Fill pie shell. Bake at 450° for 10 minutes on lowest shelf of oven. Raise to middle shelf and bake at 325° for 45 minutes, until set.

The Butternut is especially good when mashed and combined with maple syrup or orange slices, or with raisins and apple, with brandy or rum, with nutmeg or cinnamon for flavoring. Acorn has a fat, squatty shape that makes it perfect for stuffing.

Though we seem to have suggested a lot of stuffed vegetables, they do add a needed element of surprise to a meal. Onions, fruit, or sausage can be baked in the hollow of an acorn squash—or anything else that appeals to your taste buds.

October

Butternut Squash

2 medium Butternut squash
½ cup melted butter
½ cup brown sugar
1 orange
½ tsp. ginger
½ tsp. mace
¼ cup sherry

Cut squash in half. Put in pan, cover with foil and bake at 400° for 45 minutes or until tender. Scoop out pulp, removing seeds and strings. Grate rind of orange. Peel orange and cut into sections. Put squash through food mill. Beat in spices, butter, sugar, sherry and orange rind. Pile into buttered casserole. Arrange orange sections in circle on top. Bake in moderate oven until heated through.

PUMPKINS

Unfortunately the pumpkin really cannot do double duty. If he is being carved for a jack o'lantern, then he can't very well give up his flesh for a pie, pudding, or bread. That is why we grow two kinds. It is always the largest ones that are carved up anyhow, while the round and fat ones get picked off the pile one by one to be sacrificed to the god of good food.

Pumpkin can go into a lot of things besides the traditional pie, you know. Pumpkin tarts well spiced with cloves, cinnamon, and nutmeg become extra special when filmed lightly with bitey ginger marmalade. Pumpkin bread has become a favorite of some friends who ski all winter, their rather large family managing to consume six loaves on a weekend. Apparently it gives them some extra, needed energy.

Pumpkin Tarts

½ cup ginger marmalade
1 cup pumpkin, cooked and mashed
1 cup milk
2 eggs
¾ cup brown sugar
1½ tsp. cinnamon
½ tsp. ginger
¼ tsp. cloves
½ tsp. nutmeg
2 tbsp. brandy
8 tart shells, unbaked

To prepare pumpkin: Cut it in large pieces and put them in a roasting pan with about 2 inches of water in the bottom. Cover with foil and bake in a 400° oven for an hour or until pumpkin flesh is soft. Scrape out seeds and strings, saving seeds for drying. Scrape out flesh and put through a food mill. Spread a thin layer of marmalade over the bottom of each tart shell. Mix sugar and spices and add to pumpkin. Add eggs and milk and brandy. Mix well. Pour into tart shells. Bake at 450° for 10 minutes. Lower heat to 325° and bake 30 minutes or until firm.

Pumpkin Seeds

Spread pumpkin seeds over a baking sheet. Bake in a 350° oven for 30 minutes until dry and slightly puffed up. Stir frequently. Cool. Store in airtight container. Sprinkle with salt.

October

Pumpkin Bread

    1   cup white sugar
    ½   cup brown sugar
    ⅓   cup butter
    2   eggs
    1⅔ cups flour
    ¼   tsp. baking powder
    1   tsp. baking soda
    1   tsp. salt
    ½   tsp. cinnamon
    ¼   tsp. cloves
    ¼   tsp. allspice
    ⅓   cup cider or orange juice
    1   cup puréed pumpkin
    ½   cup chopped nuts (optional)

Cream sugars and butter. Add eggs, beating all. Mix dry ingredients together and stir in. Blend in cider, pumpkin, and nuts. Pour into two well-greased loaf pans. Bake at 350° for 1 hour, until bread tests done.

A pumpkin custard is somewhat reminiscent of the early days in that it uses quite a bit of the spirits and spices that were so necessary in the Colonial kitchens. One can imagine this dessert being served at Mount Vernon or Monticello.

Pumpkin Custard

    3   cups light cream
    2   cups mashed pumpkin
    ⅔   cup brown sugar
    ¼   cup rum
    6   eggs + 2 yolks
    1   tsp. salt
    1   tsp. cinnamon
    ½   tsp. ginger
    ½   tsp. nutmeg
    2   tbsp. brandy
    1   cup medium cream, whipped

Beat eggs and yolks. Scald cream and pour over beaten eggs. Beat in sugar, rum, and seasonings. Mix in pumpkin. Pour into 2-qt. casserole. Place in pan of hot water. Bake at 350° for 1¼ hours, until set. Cool at room temperature. Before serving, flame brandy over top. Serve with whipped cream.

186

October

The garden will be sleeping now, with the exception of those things we mentioned way back—chard for instance—that will be with us for part of the winter. Chard's leafy green remains a bright spot in the sere garden.

Now that the cook has a little more time, she may like to spend some of it working on particularly intriguing dinner menus. Here is such a challenging recipe which can be served without any meat accompaniment if you wish, for it holds its own very well.

Chard Rolls in Tomato Sauce

1½ lbs. chard
½ loaf French or Italian bread
1 onion, minced
1 clove garlic, minced
½ cup parsley, chopped
1 cup grated Parmesan cheese
1 cup dry bread crumbs
1 tsp. salt
  freshly ground black pepper
½ tsp. dried oregano
4 eggs
1 cup tomato sauce

Cook chard leaves. Drain and squeeze dry. Chop. Soak French bread in hot water and squeeze dry. Sauté onion and garlic in 2 tbsp. oil until limp. Do not brown. Put chard, bread, onion, and garlic through fine blade of meat grinder. Mix with the parsley, bread crumbs, salt, pepper, and oregano. Add ½ cup Parmesan cheese. Stir in eggs. Chill mixture for several hours. Shape mixture into sausage-like links with your hands which have been floured. Chill links, Bring a large pan of salted water to a full boil. Drop in links, a few at a time. Cook until they rise to the surface and are firm. Remove with skimmer and place in greased baking dish. Surround with tomato sauce. Sprinkle with ½ cup grated Parmesan cheese. Dish can be prepared ahead to this point and kept overnight. Reheat in a moderate oven.

October

JERUSALEM ARTICHOKES

The time has come to make a little more out of those strange tubers resembling sunflowers —the Jerusalem artichokes. We talked about artichokes pickle back in February.

Mrs. Rorer, in her "new" cookbook of 1902, notes that the Jerusalem artichoke does not contain any starch and therefore forms "one of the most important vegetables for diabetic patients." This fact should also appeal to all those on weight-losing diets.

Artichokes in Cream

Peel artichokes and put at once into cold water to prevent discoloration. Cut into half-inch slices and boil gently for about 20 minutes, until tender but not soft. Drain; put into serving dish and cover with heavy cream which has been heated. Sprinkle with chopped parsley.

Artichokes a la Provençale

Peel and parboil 1 lb. artichokes. Drain and cut into sizeable pieces. Heat some oil in a frying pan and add a clove of crushed garlic and 2 tbsp. minced parsley. Add artichoke pieces and sauté gently until tender. Add 1 peeled and chopped tomato. Stir all together and serve hot.

Artichoke Salad

Put peeled artichokes in cold salted water. Bring to a boil and simmer until tender but still crisp. Watch after first 10 minutes. Drain, dry, and slice. While still warm, put in bowl and add French dressing, just enough to coat each slice. Add slivered celery, chopped parsley and chives. Cover and serve at room temperature.

October

Making the garden ready for winter is a pleasant task, to be done on a crisp, clear autumn day. Pull all the remaining vines and lay them on the compost heap, if you don't till them into the soil. If you have extra hay, cover the garden with it, but be sure to mark the places where vegetables still are in the ground. The remaining carrots and the parsnips will be sweeter for a touch of frost. By now the onions, garlic, and shallots are hanging in strings in your kitchen, the last jack o'lantern has been composted, and the Indian corn is decorating the gatepost.

What do you do with that popcorn that I suggested you plant way back in the spring? Now is the time to break off the dried ears and rub them against each other over a colander placed over a bowl. In this way you will separate the kernels from the chaff. Then refrigerate the corn in covered containers. Ideally, you should not use it for a year, but let your conscience be your guide. One of the more jolly things to do with popcorn is to make nice sticky popcorn balls.

Popcorn Balls

12 cups popped popcorn
 1 cup molasses
 1 cup corn syrup
 1 tsp. vinegar
 3 tbsp. butter
 ½ tsp. salt

Cook molasses, corn syrup, and vinegar in saucepan to hard-ball stage (270°). Stir in butter and salt. Pour over popcorn in bowl, stirring with wooden spoon to cover all kernels. Butter your hands and form into balls. Set on paper to harden.

Save this project for a cold day when the garden seems far, far away and the winter stretches long, long ahead. It will start you thinking, just a little bit, about next year's garden. And of course there will be one, for many reasons.

It's human nature to want to correct mis-

189

takes, and we make some each year in our planning or planting. We put in too much of one thing, too little of another. Some vegetables we don't want to plant again, and there will be new varieties we want to try.

But perhaps the main reason we'll have other gardens is the love of growing things, the fascination of watching a simple seed develop into a perfectly formed vegetable that in turn helps our nourishment. This never-ending process we must continue, once we have started. So send for the bright new seed catalogs now, review your favorite recipes, and begin the plans for a perfect garden, until it is time to dig once again.

Index

NOTE: *Recipes and directions for table preparation are listed in italics.*

Apples, 169, *170, 171, 172,* 173
Apple trees, dwarf, 29, 31
Artichokes, Jerusalem, 34, *35,* 52, *188*
Asparagus, 15, 53, *54, 55, 56, 57*

Basil, 41, *87, 88*
Beans,
   green, 16, 40, 92, 107, *108, 109, 110*
   lima, 16, 17, *150, 151*
   pole, 17
   wax, 17, *111*
Beets, 12, 46, *83, 84,* 92, 130
Blackberries, 94, *96*
Blackberry bushes, 32, 94
Blueberries, *94, 95*
Blueberry bushes, 32, 94
Breads, fritters, muffins, *102, 153, 154, 186*
Broccoli, 19, 52, 104, *105, 106, 107*

Cabbage, 19, 52, 92, *134, 135*
   red, 19, 52, 92, *177, 178*
Cakes, cobblers,
   apple gingerbread, *170*
   blueberry, *95*
   maple, *43*
   peach, *162–3*
   plum, *165*
   sour cherry, *98*
   strawberry short, *73*
   rhubarb cobbler, *58*
Carrots, 12, 37, *38,* 46, 52, 81, *82,* 92, 130
Cauliflower, 20, 132, *133*
Celery, 20, *84, 131, 132*
Chard, Swiss, 14, *37,* 46, *187*
Cheese, recipes with, *22, 76, 78, 110, 113, 120, 126, 133, 142, 187*

Cherries, 97, *98, 99, 100, 101*
Cherry trees, dwarf, 31
Chicken, recipes with, *23–4, 59, 63, 80, 107, 156, 164, 172*
Chicken livers, recipes with, *89, 90, 123, 135, 144*
Chives, 41, *63,* 88
Chowders (see Soups)
Companion Plants (see Gardening)
Corn, 18, 19, *150,* 152, *153, 154, 155, 156, 157*
Cress, English, 48, 64
Cucumbers, 17, 18, *136, 137, 138, 139*
Currants, 96, *103*
Custard, *24, 179, 186*

Dandelion greens, 48, *49*
Dill, 110
Dressings (see Sauces)
Drinks, cordials, syllabubs, *57, 60, 73, 96, 97, 100, 163*

Eggplant, 20, 21, 139, *140, 141, 142*

Fish, *50*

Gardening,
   clean-up, 92, 182, 189
   companion plants, 35–6
   fertilizing, 34, 93
   harvesting, 10, 11, 61–2, 66, 71, 104, 130, 150, 160, 173, 182, 189
   insect pests, 35, 36, 92, 93
   location, 37
   mulching, 52, 53, 64, 92
   planning, 7, 10, 28, 33, 190
   plans, 30, 47, 64

   planting, 40, 46, 47, 48, 52, 66, 92, 107, 130
   thinning, 48
Garlic, 14
Grapes, 175, *176, 177*
Grape vines, 32–3

Ham, recipes with, *69, 110, 133, 142, 168*
Herbs, 22, 36, 40, 41, *63,* 75, *87, 88, 89,* 90
Herb cheese, *90*
Herb vinegars, *75, 87–8*

Insect pests (see Gardening)

Jams, jellies, *88,* 93, *94, 103*

Kale, 37

Lamb, recipes with, *89, 118, 140*
Leeks, 14, 21, 22, *23, 24–5*
Lemon balm, 41, 88
Lettuce, 13, 46, 48, 52, 66, 74, *76,* 92

Maple syrup, 41, *42, 43, 151*
Marjoram, 41
Meat loaf, *171*
Melons, 18, 166, *167, 168*
Mint, *60, 61, 62*
Mulching (see Gardening)

Nut trees, 28

Oregano, 41, 88
Onions, scallions, 14, 46, *143, 144, 145*
Orchard, 28, 37, 160

Parsley, 41, 48, 75
Parsnips, 13, 25, *26,* 46

Index

Pastry,
 cream filling, *74*
 pie, *162*
 tart, *74, 99*
Peaches, 160, *161, 162, 163, 164*
Peach trees, dwarf, 29, 31
Pears, 173, *174, 175*
Pear trees, dwarf, 31
Peas, 11, 40, 46, *61, 67, 68, 69,* 70, 92
Peppers, hot, 21, 52
 sweet, 21, 52, 85, *86, 157*
Pies,
 apple, *170*
 blackberry, *96*
 cherry, *98*
 grape, *176*
 leek quiche, *24–5*
 peach, *162*
 rhubarb & strawberry, *58*
 squash, *183*
Plans (see Gardening)
Plums, 164, *165, 166*
Popcorn, 15, 16, *189*
Potatoes, *146, 147, 148, 149*
Preserves, conserves, pickles, relishes,
 35, 83, 101
Pumpkins, 18, 184, *185, 186*
Pumpkin seeds, *185*

Radishes, 12, 46, 52, 130
Raspberries, 94, 96, 101, *102*
Raspberry bushes, 31–2
Rhubarb, 14, *57, 58, 59*
Rosemary, 41, 88, *89*
Rutabagas, 15, *178*

Sage, 41, *89*
Salads, *36, 57, 61,* 75, *76,* 79, *82, 84, 137,*
 149, 188
Sauces (dressings),
 Bibs Brown's, *49*
 fines herbes, *75*
 green beans, for, *110*
 hollandaise, *55*
 Maltese, *55*
 mint yoghurt, *62*
 pesto, *87*
 vinaigrette, *56,* 75
 zucchini, *119*
Sauces (sweet),
 crème fraiche, *72*
 orange, *84*
 peach, *164*
 plum, *165*
 rhubarb, *59*
 rum pot, *72*
 tutti-frutti, *72*
 walnut, *110*
Scallions (see Onions)
Shallots, 14, 64, *109, 112*
Soufflés,
 broccoli, *106*
 celery, *131*
 chard, *37*
 parsnip, *26*
 spinach, *78*
Soups, chowders,
 broccoli, *105*
 carrot, *82*
 corn & chicken, *156*
 cucumber, *136*

 pea, *61, 70*
 pistou, *22*
 potato, *149*
 tomato, *124*
 watercress cream, *50*
 zucchini, *116*
Spinach, 13, 14, 46, 77, 78, 79, 80
Squash, summer, 17, 111, *112, 113, 114,*
 115, 116, 117, 118, 119, 120, 157
 winter, 17, *183, 184*
Stews, 23–4, 81
Strawberries, 71, *72, 73, 74*
Strawberry plants, 33
Succotash, *150*

Tarragon, 41, 88, *116*
Tarts, turnovers,
 apple, *171*
 carrot, *37*
 cherry, *99*
 grape, *176–7*
 melon, *167*
 onion, *145*
 pumpkin, *185*
 strawberry, *74*
Tea, iced, *60*
Thyme, 41, 88
Tomatoes, 21, 66, 121, *122, 123, 124, 125,*
 126, 127, 157
Turnips, 15, 92, *178, 179*

Watercress, 49, *50*
Wineberries, *103*

Yoghurt, *62*

Zucchini (see Squash, summer)

641.65 B
Blanchard, Marjorie P.
Home gardener's cookbook /

CAPE FEAR COMMUNITY COLLEGE

3 3177 00053 7941